Growing
and Dividing

Growing *and* Dividing

Ellen Thro and Andrew K. Frank

**RAINTREE
STECK-VAUGHN
PUBLISHERS**

A Harcourt Company

Austin • New York
www.steck-vaughn.com

Published by Raintree Steck-Vaughn Publishers, an imprint of Steck-Vaughn Company

Developed by Discovery Books
Editor: Sabrina Crewe
Designer: Sabine Beaupré
Maps and charts: Stefan Chabluk

Raintree Steck-Vaughn Publishers Staff
Publishing Director: Walter Kossmann
Art Director: Max Brinkmann
Editor: Shirley Shalit

Library of Congress Cataloging-in-Publication Data
Thro, Ellen.
    Growing and dividing / Ellen Thro and Andrew Frank.
        p. cm. -- (The making of America)
    Includes bibliographical references and index.
    ISBN 0-8172-5704-7
        1. United States--History--1815-1861--Juvenile literature. 2. United States--Territorial
    expansion--Juvenile literature. 3. United States--History--Civil War,
    1861-1865--Causes--Juvenile literature. [1. United States--History--1815-1861. 2. United
    States--Territorial expansion. 3. United States--History--Civil War, 1861-1865--Causes.]
    I. Frank, Andrew, 1970- II. Title. III. Making of America (Austin, Tex.)
    E338.T48 2000
    973.5--dc21

                                                                                00-034163

Printed and bound in the United States of America
1 2 3 4 5 6 7 8 9 0 IP 04 03 02 01 00

Acknowledgments
Cover The Granger Collection; pp. 6, 11, 12, 13, 14, 16 Corbis; pp. 20, 24 The Granger Collection; pp. 27, 28 (both) Corbis; pp. 29, 31 The Granger Collection; pp. 33, 35, 37 Corbis; p. 38 The Granger Collection; pp. 39, 41, 42 Corbis; p. 44 The Granger Collection; pp. 49, 51, 53, 54 Corbis; p. 55 The Granger Collection; p. 57 Corbis; pp. 60, 62 The Granger Collection; pp. 63, 65, 66, 67, 70, 71, 72, 74, 75 Corbis; p. 77 The Granger Collection; p. 78 Corbis; p. 79 The Granger Collection; pp. 81, 82, 83 Corbis.

Cover illustration: This lithograph from 1860 shows Illinois Senator Daniel Webster addressing the United States Senate in 1850 during the great debate on slavery, the Constitution, and the Union.

Contents

Introduction

In the War of 1812, when the United States fought Britain, Americans defended the independence they had declared in the American Revolution. By winning the war, the United States became the major power in North America. The Treaty of Ghent, which officially ended the war, brought in what many Americans of the time called the "Era of Good Feelings." The nation's territory and population grew, and national prosperity grew as well.

By 1820, the American economy was booming. At the same time, two distinct regions developed within the nation. These regions were the North and the South. Both experienced economic growth, but of different kinds. In the Southern states, cotton, rice, and tobacco plantations flourished, and so did the slavery system on which these depended. In the Northern states, commerce and new manufacturing industries expanded rapidly.

The time between the end of the War of 1812 and the beginning of the Civil War in 1861 is known as the antebellum (meaning "before the war") period. During this era, there were many disagreements in national government and among the population as a whole. Although Northern textile mills and Southern cotton plantations needed each other to prosper, the tensions between the regions were impossible to ignore. As the nation grew, so did the political divisions and hostility between the North and the South.

The early settlers in the Southern colonies that later became the states of North Carolina, South Carolina, and Georgia worked cotton and tobacco plantations. By 1820, many cotton plantations, like the one below, had moved west to the fertile lands along the Mississippi River.

1

Two Regions and One Nation

Although most people in the North still lived as farmers in 1820, the region seemed destined to have a different future. As the century progressed, more Northerners worked in textile mills, in banks, and in commerce. New types of machines increased factory production, and newly-built canals and railroads brought goods and services across the region.

The South also flourished in antebellum America. Unlike the North, which grew through modernization and industry, the South still relied on staple crops to fuel its economic growth. Farmers acquired more land to increase production, and growing numbers of slaves provided most of the region's manual labor.

Cotton

The prosperity of the antebellum South owed much to Eli Whitney's invention of the cotton gin in 1783. This machine allowed cotton to be processed quickly and inexpensively, and soon cotton became a seemingly limitless product. One machine could separate the hard, rough seeds from 1,000 pounds (450 kg) of cotton in a single day, many times more than the amount that could be cleaned by hand. The cotton gin, along with increasing demand for the product in Britain, brought an economic boom to the antebellum South. The region's reliance on cotton became so great that the South became known as the Cotton Kingdom.

The Cotton Kingdom was born in South Carolina and Georgia, where cotton had been grown for many years. It would not remain confined to these Southeastern states for long. Almost immediately after the cotton gin became available, Southern planters moved farther inland with their African slaves. Soon, Alabama and Mississippi became the center of the nation's cotton crop. And by the 1840s, cotton farming stretched as far west as Texas.

The westward migration of American settlements in the South was slow but steady throughout the eighteenth century. In the early nineteenth century, the pace of the migration increased. Southerners eyed lands to the west of their region with optimism and greed. They saw them as potential cotton fields. This meant trouble for the Indians who had lived on these lands for generations. White Southerners demanded that politicians arrange the purchase of Indian lands, and the politicians obliged. By the 1830s, most Southeastern Indians had been forcibly moved west by the government.

Slavery

The growth of cotton agriculture resulted in the expanded use of African slaves, who were brought from Africa by slave traders and sold to plantation owners. Southern whites took their slaves wherever they planted their cotton. Slaves cleared land, planted and tended to the fields, cleaned, cooked, mended fences, and performed countless other tasks. The economic boom of the South could not have occurred without the labor of millions of slaves.

The expansion of the Cotton Kingdom was accompanied by huge growth in the slave population. In 1790, there were nearly 700,000 slaves in the United States. In 1800, the slave population had increased to a million. From 1808, the slave trade, or bringing slaves from foreign countries, was outlawed. Even so, by 1860, the nation contained nearly 4 million slaves. These were people who had been born into slavery in the United States, the descendants of those who had been brought originally from Africa.

Slave owners, often called masters, employed a variety of punishments to keep their slaves in line. They used the whip,

"It was never too hot or too cold; it could never rain, blow hail, or snow, too hard for us to work in the field. Work, work, work, was scarcely more the order of the day than of the night."

Frederick Douglass, former slave, Narrative of the Life of Frederick Douglass

and the threat of the whip, to push their slaves to work longer and harder. Masters frequently branded their slaves to mark them as property. They also withheld food, separated families, and used other cruel punishments. Many slave owners hired white overseers to keep track of the slaves during the day. Others used black slave drivers to watch over their slaves.

Slaves had no rights under Southern law, and throughout most of the antebellum era, the North also offered few legal protections to slaves. Slaves were considered the chattels, or personal property, of their masters. They could be bought, sold, punished, moved, and branded as if they were animals. Thomas Ruffin, a member of the North Carolina Supreme Court, made this position clear when he stated in 1829 that

The Life of a Southern Slave

Slaves lived in various environments in the antebellum South, with most working as field hands on plantations. But they were also coachmen, blacksmiths, and household servants both on plantations and in cities.

In the South Carolina rice fields, slaves were usually given a list of tasks to finish each day or week. If the slaves worked quickly, they could earn free time for themselves. Many used this time to learn new skills or to grow vegetables in their own gardens. Sometimes they made money from the things they produced. On the larger cotton plantations, masters organized their slaves into gangs of workers. These slaves worked as a group and were closely supervised. Gangs worked from sunup to sundown. In addition to working in the fields, slave women cooked, cleaned, did laundry, sewed, and cared for the plantation's white and black children.

Many slaves never set foot on a plantation or farm. They lived in the South's towns and small cities. Some worked at ironworks, others mined gold or coal. In western Virginia, slaves worked in the salt industry.

Wherever they lived, slaves created communities of their own. During the evenings, these slaves often enjoyed each other's company in song, prayer, and dance. As one slave recalled, "From sunup to sundown we belonged to master; but from sundown to sunup we were our own."

"the power of the master must be absolute to render the submission of the slave perfect."

Despite their position, Southern slaves created strong families and lively communities. Their backgrounds were varied because slaves had originally been brought from many different African communities with their own languages and traditions. Slave culture reflected these diverse backgrounds as well as the American culture in which they lived.

Southern slaves frequently married, even though the law declared that these relationships were unofficial and subject to the wishes of the master. Some masters consented to slave marriages because marriage encouraged childbirth and created a steady workforce. In most Southern states, laws prevented slaves from receiving an education. A few slaves did learn to read and write, but in 1860 only about 5 percent of them could sign their own name.

Industry in the South

A few Southern whites hoped that their region could grow through industry, not just agriculture. However, for most of the early nineteenth century, slave owners found it more profitable to use their slaves on farms than in cities. Many white Southerners resisted change in their traditional economy. Others just thought that industrialization would disturb the rural lifestyle they preferred.

Because of this, the South experienced little urban or industrial growth. Port cities—like New Orleans, Savannah, and Charleston—grew quite large because they provided places to export and import goods. They rarely, however experienced the development of large industries or factories. (One notable exception was the Tredegar ironworks in Richmond that opened in 1836, where as many as 7,000 slaves worked.) Nevertheless, the antebellum South prospered since it provided much of the nation's raw materials. And Southern farmers often looked to Northern banks for loans and relied as well on Northern merchants to buy and sell their goods.

"I would ten thousand times rather that my children should be the half-starved paupers of Ireland than to be the most pampered among the slaves of America."

Harriet Jacobs, former slave, Incidents in the Life of a Slave Girl, Written by Herself

White Southern Society

Southern society contained a small number of powerful planters who owned more than 20 slaves. Although these planters made up only 2 percent of the white population in the South, they owned half of the region's slaves. They filled most elected positions on local, state, and federal (or national) levels. They were justices of the peace, church leaders, judges, congressmen, senators, and some became United States presidents.

Not all white Southerners, however, were planters. Most Southern farmers were members of what was called the yeomanry. Yeoman farmers were neither rich nor poor, but they owned their own land and were scattered all over the countryside. They grew much of the food that they ate and bought only what they could not produce for themselves. Many yeoman farmers raised cattle, hogs, and chickens. Some grew small amounts of cotton, tobacco, or other marketable items. They usually owned at the most one or two slaves.

Charleston was one of the cities in the South that grew as the cotton industry boomed. The wharves where the cotton was loaded onto ships in the harbor (above) were busy places.

11

Southern society also contained a poor, white, landless community. Most poor whites hired themselves out as laborers or struggled to find a trade. Members of this group often lived on the margins of society, surviving on Indian lands or other lands not yet settled by whites. There, on the edges of the South, they worked as trappers, hunters, and herders.

Industry in the North

Meanwhile, the North was undergoing great industrial changes, resulting partly from the cotton boom in the South. Before the cotton boom, Southern planters exported most of their cotton to Britain. In 1807, Congress passed the Embargo Act. This law prevented American ships from entering foreign ports and forced Southern planters to find an alternative market for their cotton.

Merchants in the North met this demand by developing their own textile industry. After the embargo ended in 1809, the New England textile industry continued to grow. By 1815, there were over 60 times as many cotton-spinning machines in the region's factories as there had been in 1807. The demand for cotton continued to increase and Northern textile mills increased their production to match it.

This power loom, which ran on steam, wove cotton threads into calico cloth. Power looms enabled factories to produce huge quantities of cloth and turned the Northern textile industry into a booming business in the mid-1800s.

A further increase in production was made possible by the invention of the power loom. The machine's use of waterpower, and later steam, transformed the industry. A textile mill in Waltham, Massachusetts, was the first to use the power loom. Its effects were staggering. It raised the mill's annual production of cloth from 4 million yards (3.6 million meters) in 1817 to 308 million yards (277 million meters) in 1837. Soon after its introduction, mills across New England enjoyed similar successes.

New Inventions in Antebellum America

Traditionally, manufacturing depended on a supply of water, which was used to turn the wheels that powered mills and small factories. The invention of advanced steam engines during the early nineteenth century freed the factory from the river. Steam powered the new textile looms and other industrial machines, as well as steamboats and the steam engines that pulled trains.

In the 1850s, William Kelly from Kentucky invented a process for turning iron to steel by running an air current through molten iron. A similar process was invented in England at about the same time. The Bessemer-Kelly process allowed the mass production of steel in large factories and turned the city of Pittsburgh, Pennsylvania, into a major manufacturing center.

Many other inventions transformed American life in the antebellum era. These included:

- The telegraph: A method of instant long-distance communication that sent electrical pulses along wires, perfected by Samuel F. B. Morse in 1832.
- The steel plow: A tool strong enough to turn the heavy prairie soils, perfected by John Deere in 1837.
- The reaper: A mechanical harvesting machine for large-scale farming, invented by Cyrus H. McCormick in 1831.
- The sewing machine: A machine that made sewing faster and easier than by hand, invented by Elias Howe in 1846.
- The safety pin: Invented by Walter Hunt in 1849.
- The revolver: An accurate hand pistol capable of firing several shots without reloading, patented by Samuel Colt in 1835.
- Vulcanization of rubber: A chemical treatment of rubber to make it harder and resistant to heat and cold, invented by Charles Goodyear in 1839.
- The typewriter: Invented by Charles Thurber in 1843.
- The passenger elevator: Invented by Elisha Otis in 1852.

The first Singer sewing machine, sold in 1851.

During the nineteenth century, manufacturing machines replaced hand labor in many factories. Lathes, which shaped a piece of wood by rotating it past a fixed blade, automated furniture manufacturing. Nails and screws were no longer made by hand as machines could now cut them automatically.

Mass Production

The movement away from small, home industry and toward mass production also transformed American manufacturing. Eli Whitney, the inventor of the cotton gin, introduced the most essential element of mass production: interchangeable parts. In mass production, workers specialized in making one part of the final product. Other workers then put the parts together. This was more efficient than craftsmen who built an entire item or range of items from start to finish. Mass-produced products soon became commonplace in America. Samuel Colt, for example, used mass production to build a new type of gun called the "six-shooter." Like the Colt six-shooter, mass-produced Waltham watches, Singer sewing machines, and Remington rifles all became household names.

Northern farmers also benefited from new technology. They used mass-produced reapers to harvest their grain. These machines could cut more than 12 acres in a single day, five times the amount an average field hand could cut with a handheld scythe. With these machines, Northern farms became more productive. Fewer farm workers could now harvest greater quantities of wheat. Soon, the United States would become the world's main wheat provider, or "bread basket."

Roads and Stagecoaches

New forms of transportation and communications also made a huge impact in the North. They allowed people, products, and information to travel faster and for greater

"Every new and useful machine, invented and improved, confers a general benefit upon all classes—the poor as well as the rich."

Article in the Scientific American, 1851

The original revolver, or "six-shooter," was patented by Samuel Colt in 1835. The revolving chamber held six bullets that could be discharged one after the other without reloading the gun.

distances. Roads, canals, railroads, steamboats, and the telegraph altered the United States as a whole, but in particular they transformed the Northeast and Midwest.

Toll-charging turnpike roads were built as early as 1790 in the United States. These roads allowed heavy wagons to be pulled across the eastern mountains. The National Road, which started in Cumberland, Maryland, only reached Wheeling, Virginia, in 1818. By 1850, it stretched from Baltimore, Maryland, to Vandalia, Illinois.

Commercial stagecoach lines connected many cities in the Northeast, although in the South there were few stagecoach lines. The trips were still slow and exhausting, but Americans who did not own their own coaches could now travel between the nation's major cities. From New York City, it took about 36 hours to reach Boston and 24 hours to reach Philadelphia.

Canals and Steamboats

Many turnpikes connected with natural and man-made waterways. The benefits of water transportation were many, not least of which were speed and reliability. The man-made waterways joined lakes and rivers, and allowed boats to transport wheat and other crops from the Midwest to the commercial centers and shipping ports in the East. The canals were popular for transporting people only for about ten years, when the railroads replaced them, but they remained essential for the transportation of farm products.

Of the many canals built throughout the nation, the most important was the Erie Canal in New York. It took people and manufactured goods west and agricultural products east. After the construction of the Erie Canal, Americans built hundreds of waterways in the hope of achieving an economic boom similar to that experienced in upstate New York. Most of these canals were built in the Northeast and the Midwest.

The steamboat, another antebellum invention, made the canals even more important. Robert Fulton introduced the first successful steamboat, the *Clermont*, in 1807. Steamboats

The Erie Canal

Some people believe the famous Erie Canal was responsible for the economic growth experienced in antebellum America. The Erie Canal was built between 1817 and 1825. It ran between Albany and Buffalo, New York, a distance of 363 miles (580 km). When it was built, the waterway was the longest canal in the world. It allowed boats to travel from New York City to Minnesota: Boats could begin on the Hudson River, continue on the Erie Canal to Lake Erie, and then end up on Lake Superior in Minnesota after traveling through Lake Huron.

The Erie Canal was the biggest governmental engineering project in the world at the time. The canal cut through forests and swamps and required millions of cubic yards of soil and rocks to be moved by hand. Many of the workers who built the canal were Irish immigrants who worked 12-hour days for only 80 cents a day. The canal had 83 locks, a series of "steps" that raised and lowered boats as they passed from one water level to another. It also had 18 aqueducts, the bridges that carried canals across rivers.

Barges were slowly pulled by teams of horses that walked on the towpath next to the waterway. It took about four days for a trip between New York City and Buffalo. Still, it was the fastest and cheapest way to go. Wagon transportation cost $100 a ton from New York to Buffalo in 1817; a boat on the Erie could transport the same load for about $8.

Eventually, the canal became part of the New York Barge Canal, which is still used. Today, the New York State Thruway (Interstate 90) parallels the old canal's route. Sections of the old canal can still be seen: The Erie Canal Park in Camillus, New York, has seven miles (11 km) of original canal and towpath.

The Erie Canal in the 1840s.

could travel upstream easily and did not rely, as sailboats did, on unreliable winds for power. For several years, however, the shallow waters of most waterways made the use of steamboats impractical. Only small boats could travel most rivers and canals before Americans began to dig trenches to deepen the waterways. Furthermore, for several years, coal remained too expensive a fuel to use for steamboats.

By the 1820s, engineers changed the shape of steamboats and turned them into the main means of transportation on the Ohio and Mississippi Rivers. About a dozen steamboats were in operation in 1815, but by 1860 there were over 3,000 transporting people, machinery, and goods on the nation's rivers and canals.

Railroads and the Growth of Cities

By 1850, the railroad had become the most important form of transportation. The United States' 9,000 miles (14,400 km) of track in 1850 was the most of any country. Ten years later, the nation contained a staggering 30,000 miles (48,000 km). Two-thirds of these tracks were in the Northern states and Midwest. The expansion of the railroad transformed the North. The rapid construction of railroads provided an extensive system of tracks that connected towns with cities.

Cities emerged wherever the railroads met each other or forms of water transportation. These transportation junctions became industrial and commercial centers because they attracted wealthy businessmen who built grain storehouses, flour mills, docks, banks, shops, insurance companies, and textile mills. Because of new industries and commerce, St. Louis, Missouri, and Chicago grew to become large cities.

Some of this growth resulted from waves of immigrants coming to the United States and finding jobs in factories. Most immigrants had fled the poverty of their European farms. Few of them wished or had the money to purchase or rent farmland, and they remained primarily in the cities. Northeastern cities also attracted American farmers who saw wage labor as an alternative to agriculture.

"Some imagined it to be a sea-monster, whilst others did not hesitate to express the belief that it was a sign of the approaching judgment."

Resident of Poughkeepsie, New York, about the Clermont steamboat, 1807

By 1860, a network of roads, canals, and railroads had spread across the eastern part of North America. Cities grew rapidly along these routes, and new towns sprang up at major junctions.

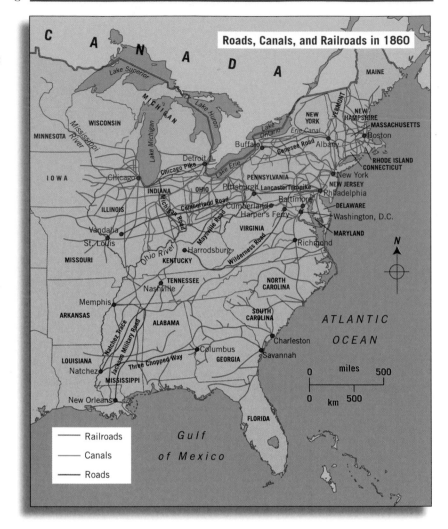

Roads, Canals, and Railroads in 1860

In the eighteenth century, Boston and Philadelphia were the centers of the nation's commerce. By the 1830s, New York had taken that position, due mainly to the Erie Canal. Its population was over 200,000 (not counting Brooklyn, which was then a separate city). New York also grew to be the nation's economic capital, as it became the base of many banks and other financial institutions.

Some New Yorkers made fortunes in trade and built mansions in new neighborhoods. But large numbers of poor immigrants, mainly Irish and German, also made the city their home. New York became the place from which people and finished products moved west, and to which raw materials arrived from the Midwest.

During the antebellum era, the small Northern cities of the nation's early years began to look more like modern big cities. They had large factories, many small businesses, and both rich and poor neighborhoods. People traveled on mass transit, and streetcars pulled by horses clogged the streets.

The Rise and Fall of American Railroads

In the 1830s, the railroad became the most important form of long-distance transportation in the United States. The "iron horse," as the railroad was called, was faster, cheaper, and more reliable than the system of stagecoaches that it replaced.

Before the Civil War, most rail lines were in the North and East. The South built railroads of its own, but not with the same success. It had far fewer miles of tracks and most areas were out of reach of the railroads. And railroad lines in the South had tracks that differed in width from line to line. This made it necessary to move goods from one train to another as they traveled across the region. The South did not adopt the standard track size that was used in the antebellum North until 1886.

After the Civil War, American railroads continued to grow. In 1868, the Union Pacific and Central Pacific Railroads united their lines in Utah, allowing trains to go from coast to coast for the first time. The renewed growth of the railroad resulted in over 164,000 miles (263,900 km) of line being laid by 1890. Improved engines, new bridges, and larger trains all made the railroad the most convenient and inexpensive way to travel.

This continued into the twentieth century, when two new inventions reduced the importance of the railroad in America. The automobile, first successfully operated in 1893, allowed people in the following century to travel farther and more cheaply. The United States and local governments built highways across the nation, and commuters turned to their cars instead of the trains. The invention of the airplane in 1903 made long-distance travel even cheaper. Although freight goods are still transported by rail, the airplane has overtaken the railroad as a means of transporting goods and people over long distances.

2

New Ideas in Daily Life

Some revival meetings of the 1800s took the form of camps, where worshipers and preachers from a number of churches would join others of their own religion for large gatherings. The fiery preachers would whip up their audiences into a state of religious frenzy.

A merica was changing, and for some these changes were coming too fast and creating too much disorder. Some Americans came to believe that the modern world was out of control and that their job was to create order.

The Revival of Religion

One response to these concerns was a wave of religious changes that spread through the United States between 1820 and 1850, as people renewed their interest in spiritual life. Preachers held services outside and in tents, to help people

directly experience God's spirit and turn away from the modern ways that they saw around them. Many Protestant groups, especially Baptists, Methodists, and Presbyterians, grew during this period.

New religious movements also appeared. Unitarianism, which was founded in 1819, attracted leading writers and thinkers, like Ralph Waldo Emerson, and was influential in New England's cultural life. A religious group called Perfectionists (now known as Pentecostals) also emerged in antebellum America. Its members believed that they were communicating directly with the Holy Spirit. Seventh Day Adventism and Mormonism also began in these decades.

Some churches split apart. African Americans, for example, separated from older churches and founded their own denominations, including the African Methodist Episcopal Church. Reform Judaism also emerged as an alternative to more traditional forms of the Jewish religion.

Other religious groups split apart over the issue of slavery. As antislavery feeling grew in the North, some Southerners believed that they needed religious organizations of their own. The Southern Baptists split from the national Baptist Church in 1843, and the Southern Methodists split from their national Church in 1844. The Presbyterians divided in the 1840s and 1850s to form Northern and Southern branches.

Immigrants from Europe

A huge change in American society and ideas was brought about by the arrival of many European immigrants. Irish, German, and Russian immigrants flooded Northern cities. These newcomers helped New York's population grow from 312,000 in 1840 to 805,000 in 1860. In the same 20 years, Philadelphia's population rose over 250 percent and Boston's population nearly doubled. In the 1850s, foreign-born residents outnumbered native-born Americans in St. Louis, Missouri; Chicago, Illinois; and Milwaukee, Wisconsin.

At the same time as the immigrants flooded in, American cities experienced an increase in the crime rate. Murders,

"The lust of accumulation has ever been the root of much evil among men."

The Christian Examiner, *July 1837*

21

This chart shows the main groups of European immigrants that arrived in the United States in the first half of the nineteenth century. The dramatic increase in the number of Irish who came in the 1840s and 1850s was due to the Potato Famine in Ireland. People left in the thousands to avoid starvation in their homeland.

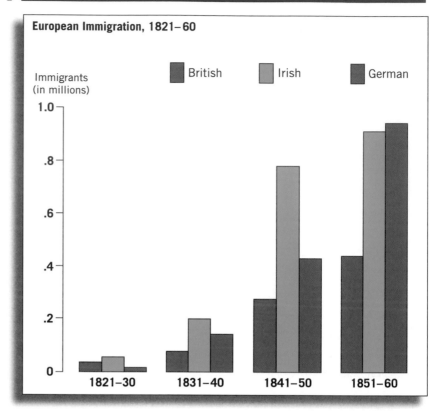

European Immigration, 1821–60

theft, and other crimes increased in poor neighborhoods. Immigrants, usually arriving without money or the prospect of a job, occasionally stole food to feed families. Others were arrested for being homeless, a condition which nineteenth-century America called the crime of "vagrancy."

In part, the apparent increase in crime was a result of the fears of white, native-born Americans. They became scared when the city filled with people who spoke languages other than English, wore clothing that seemed strange, and otherwise behaved in foreign ways. This led America's major cities to hire increasing numbers of professional police officers, which in turn led to more arrests.

Some Americans blamed immigrants for the disorders in the city: not only crime, but pollution and overcrowding. The rise of foreign-born voters, politicians, and workers also angered native-born Americans who saw immigrants take away their political power and their jobs. The Nativist

Irish Immigrants

Between 1815 and 1860, over 5 million immigrants entered the United States. At least 2 million of these newcomers came from Ireland. In 1851, about 250,000 Irish immigrants arrived in the United States. They were America's largest immigrant group by far in the 1840s.

Most of these people came to America to escape the Irish Potato Famine. The potato blight, a disease that destroyed 40 percent of the crop, struck in 1845 and returned several times in the following years. At the time of the famine, about 4 million poor Irishmen, women, and children relied on potatoes as their main food source. The famine killed nearly a million people, and left most of the country sick and hungry.

Irish people, desperate to escape starvation, boarded ships bound for America. But sickness spread rapidly aboard the ships, and even more of them died before ever reaching their destination. So many Irish people, about one in six, perished on the journeys across the Atlantic that the ships they traveled in became known as "coffin ships." The passengers who survived arrived penniless in the United States, hoping for a new start in life. They settled mainly in Northeastern and Midwestern cities. There, the Irish newcomers faced prejudice because they were not just foreigners, but Catholics in a mostly Protestant society. Over the years, however, Irish communities grew and became an important part of the workforce and culture, especially in New York and Boston.

movement, composed mainly of white Protestants, emerged to meet this so-called "immigrant problem." They attacked Catholics, Jews, Asians, blacks, and any other non-English foreigners. Nativists occasionally inspired violence, such as the burning of a Catholic convent in Charlestown, Massachusetts, in 1834.

The Nativists supported the American, or Know-Nothing, political party and became linked to the Republican party in the late 1850s. The Know-Nothing party, formed in the 1850s, was anti-immigrant and anti-Catholic, and wanted to ban all newcomers and Catholics from voting. It was called "Know-Nothing" because when members were questioned

Anti-Catholic feeling among the Nativists led to scenes of angry violence, such as this one in Philadelphia in 1844. The Nativists in their tall beaver hats are seen throwing bricks and firing guns at the local militiamen who tried to prevent their attacks on immigrants.

about it, they were supposed to state only that "I know nothing." Nativists led the Republicans to take a stand against immigration, but their power was felt more in local politics than nationally.

Social Reforms

The arrival of large numbers of European immigrants resulted in changes in schooling. Some Americans wondered if the newcomers could learn to take part in the United States' democratic society. Free public schools under state supervision opened in large numbers, and helped foreigners learn to become Americans and to speak English.

Americans with mental illnesses received new forms of assistance in the nineteenth century. Before then, "insane asylums" had been dumping grounds for the mentally ill. Dorothea Dix was a pioneer in bringing them better medical care. She first saw mentally ill people in jail with criminals. Dix then inspected insane asylums in Massachusetts and described the horrible conditions in a report to the state legislature in 1843. During the next three years, she visited more than 500 asylums, jails, and poorhouses in other states. Dix founded, enlarged, or improved state-supported mental hospitals in 15 states, and in Canada and England.

Utopian Communities

Starting in the 1840s, a few Americans sought to reform their society by creating small utopian, or ideal, communities. These people believed in self-reliance, or being responsible for oneself, and also in a rural and farm-based lifestyle. Many belonged to the Transcendentalists, a religious and philosophical group of the period. Transcendentalists believed that people were connected to nature in a spiritual way. The communities would, they hoped, provide escape from the modern world and industrial life.

The first utopian communities were small, agricultural, and religious in nature. They rarely lasted more than a few years. Brook Farm, in Massachusetts, was one of the most famous of these communities, but it lasted only from 1841 to 1847. A successful utopian community was the North American Phalanx, in Red Bank, New Jersey. This community, which lasted from 1844 to 1855, was influenced by the French reformer Charles Fourier. Like the two dozen other projects influenced by Fourier, it tried to replace the economic competition that existed in American society with communal, or group, ownership of property.

A different kind of utopia was designed by a Welsh reformer, Robert Owen. His communities were factory towns that combined farming and manufacturing industries. Owen emphasized practical improvements, such as better sanitation, housing, and schools. Stores provided goods the residents needed, and were not supposed to make a profit. Owen's most famous community was at New Harmony, Indiana.

The Temperance Movement

The temperance, or anti-alcohol, movement began in the early 1800s. It was a response to increased crime, bad health, poverty, and lower moral standards, all of which temperance supporters believed were caused by drinking alcoholic beverages. The Methodist Church began supporting temperance in 1816, and the American Temperance Union held its first annual convention in 1836.

"We meant to lessen the laboring man's great burden of toil, by performing our due share of it. . . . We sought our profit by mutual aid. . . . And, as the basis of our institution, we purposed to offer up the earnest toil of our bodies, as a prayer no less than an effort for the advancement of our race."

Nathaniel Hawthorne, writing about a utopian community in his novel The Blithedale Romance

American Writers

The 1800s saw the appearance of many important American authors. These writers relied on American themes and events for their stories. Washington Irving became known for tales set along the Hudson River in New York. He wrote *Rip Van Winkle* and *The Legend of Sleepy Hollow* between 1820 and 1840. At about the same time, James Fenimore Cooper wrote exciting novels about the western wilderness. His novels include *The Last of the Mohicans*, *The Deerslayer*, and *The Pathfinder*.

Many Boston-based writers were members of a large community of thinkers of the 1830s and 1840s. They were part of what is called the New England Renaissance, or cultural rebirth. One of the leaders was Ralph Waldo Emerson, the philosopher who popularized Transcendentalism. Emerson's essays "Self-Reliance" and "Nature" explained his beliefs. Henry David Thoreau was another Transcendentalist, who described his philosophy in essays and books. He is best known for *Walden*, which he wrote after a year living alone on Walden Pond.

Edgar Allan Poe is known as the father of American science fiction and mystery stories. His stories and poems, still popular today, include "The Gold Bug," "The Cask of Amontillado," and "The Raven."

Most people, however, did not rely on the giants of American literature for entertainment. Popular novels, museums, and the "penny press" provided daily amusement for millions. Newspapers of the "penny press" focused on the sensational and, unlike the traditional papers, were aimed at immigrants and working-class Americans. The first "dime novel," a book which sold cheaply to attract poorer readers, was published in 1860. Written by Ann Sophia Stephens, *Malaeska: The Indian Wife of the White Hunter* was a best-seller, and sold 300,000 copies in its first year.

Enthusiastic public speakers like John Bartholomew Gough converted thousands of followers. Millions of people read temperance novels. One best-seller was *Ten Nights in a Barroom and What I Saw There*, by Timothy Shay Arthur. Published in 1854, it sold a million copies by 1860. The novel was turned into a play and drew large audiences for decades. Arthur, like many Americans, believed that most social evils were caused by alcoholism.

Temperance reformers did not only try to convince Americans to stop drinking. They also tried to pass laws that banned the sale of liquor. In the 1840s, Neal Dow, the mayor of Portland, Maine, led a national campaign to pass laws prohibiting the sale of liquor. Maine passed the law in 1846. By 1855, 12 more states and one territory had passed similar laws.

This cartoon from about 1820 shows how the temperance reformers viewed alcohol. They believed it was responsible for social evils, such as murder and the spread of disease, as shown by the labels on the barrels.

The Women's Rights Movement

Some of the most vocal reformers in antebellum America fought for women's rights. Four of the early leaders of this early nineteenth-century movement were Frances Wright, a Scottish immigrant; Maria Stewart, who was black; and Angelina Grimké and her sister Sarah Grimké, who were white Southern Quakers. These women lectured to audiences of both men and women, whites and blacks. Such audiences were a rarity at the time.

During the nineteenth century, American women had few legal rights. They could not vote or hold elected office. If they were married, they could not even own property. Not many women received higher education, as most colleges refused to admit them as students. The few that studied medicine or law privately were barred from joining the professional societies that made it legal to practice.

For the most part, Americans believed that women belonged in the home, raising children and caring for the house. Many women accepted these domestic roles. Others accepted them, but they expanded their influence outside the home by becoming active in reform movements. By 1840, half of the members of antislavery organizations were women.

"I have heard much about the sexes being equal; I can carry as much as any man, and can eat as much too, if I can get it. I am as strong as any man."

Sojourner Truth, abolitionist and supporter of women's rights, 1851

27

Lucretia Coffin Mott (1793–1880) and Elizabeth Cady Stanton (1815–1902)

Lucretia Coffin Mott

Lucretia Coffin Mott and Elizabeth Cady Stanton were leading feminists and social reformers. Both fought to bring equality and suffrage to American women.

Mott and Stanton together organized the first women's rights meeting, which was held in Seneca Falls, New York, in 1848. Both Mott and Stanton signed the meeting's "Declaration of Sentiments." After the Seneca Falls meeting, Mott and Stanton continued to try and reform American society. In 1850, Mott published *Discourse on Women*, which discussed women's lack of political rights in Europe and America. After the Civil War, she worked to gain African Americans the right to vote.

Elizabeth Cady Stanton

Stanton focused most of her attention on achieving equality for women in America. In 1852, she became allied with another feminist, Susan B. Anthony. The two led the women's movement for several decades. Stanton was president of the National Woman Suffrage Association from 1862 to 1890 and of the National American Woman Suffrage Association from 1890 to 1892. An outstanding speaker and writer, Stanton was also the editor of a feminist magazine, the *Resolution*, from 1868 to 1870. She wrote several books, including the story of her life, *Eighty Years and More*.

However, these movements were mainly led by men. To overcome this, some women formed their own temperance and antislavery organizations. Others took a more direct approach. They formed organizations to gain more legal rights for themselves.

Seneca Falls

In the 1840s, Elizabeth Cady Stanton and Lucretia Coffin Mott, already active in social reform, emerged as important women's rights campaigners. Stanton and her husband were on their honeymoon in London, England, in 1840. There, they attended an international antislavery, or abolitionist, meeting. Attending as well were Lucretia Coffin Mott and her husband James Mott, both prominent abolitionists. Lucretia Mott was also a well-known lecturer on temperance and the rights of working people as well as on abolition. But the convention refused to let the women speak, in spite of their experience. Mott and Stanton decided to fight back. They began to plan the first major women's rights meeting in the United States.

In 1848, about 300 women met in Seneca Falls, in northern New York, to form a national organization that demanded more equality for women in business and employment. They gathered in the Wesley Methodist Church where they wrote a "Declaration of Sentiments and Resolutions," a reworking of the Declaration of Independence. A number of men also attended, and James Mott led some of the sessions. The Declaration, signed by one-third of the people present, stated that "all men and women are created equal" and that women also had "inalienable rights." It listed 16 areas of life where women were denied equal rights. Suffrage, or the right to vote, was the most important privilege that was denied to women. The Declaration of Sentiments also demanded equal rights for women in marriage, education, religion, employment, and politics.

> ". . . because women do feel themselves aggrieved, oppressed, and fraudulently deprived of their most sacred rights, we insist that they have immediate admission to all the rights and privileges which belong to them as citizens of these United States."
>
> *From the "Declaration of Sentiments," Seneca Falls, New York, 1848*

Elizabeth Cady Stanton addresses the women's rights convention at Seneca Falls in 1848. It was the first time women and men had gathered together in large numbers to declare that equality for women was an issue that needed to be addressed.

The meeting at Seneca Falls is acknowledged as the start of a long struggle for women's equality in America. Women would not obtain the right to vote in federal elections until the Nineteenth Amendment to the Constitution was ratified in 1920. However, the Declaration of Sentiments rejected the belief that women should remain in the "domestic sphere."

Women's Rights

The women's rights movement was originally linked with the abolition of slavery and equal rights for black people. When the Fifteenth Amendment gave blacks the right to vote, many women protested that it ignored women. Female suffrage on the national level finally came in 1920 with the Nineteenth Amendment.

During the following decades, the women's movement remained rather quiet. In the 1960s, it experienced a revival. In part, this renewed spirit resulted from the publication of Betty Friedan's *The Feminine Mystique* in 1963. This best-seller challenged the widespread belief that women belonged in the home. At the same time, the struggle of blacks to achieve civil rights provided an example for women's rights. Millions of women joined in the new fight for equality, and Congress listened. In 1964, it passed a law prohibiting employment discrimination on the basis of race, sex, religion, or national origin. This ended one of the major legal barriers to equality between women and men.

In 1966, the National Organization of Women (NOW) formed to fight for equality in all aspects of American life. NOW's decision to push for the Equal Rights Amendment (ERA) resulted in a conservative backlash. The ERA simply stated that "Equality of rights under the law should not be denied or abridged by the United States or any State on account of sex." The amendment received the support of Congress in 1972, but only 30 states (eight states short of the required number) ratified it. It was never passed and, in many ways, this signaled the end of the women's movement. In the years that followed, most Americans believed the movement had become too extreme, and many women stopped calling themselves feminists. Current American law recognizes the legal equality of women, but they continue to earn less than men in many areas of work.

3

The Struggle Against Slavery

There was an issue in antebellum America that rose above all others in dividing the nation. Until the 1820s, the struggle against slavery was fought mostly by slaves and former slaves themselves. As the 1800s progressed, more and more white Northerners joined black people in the fight against the South's "peculiar institution."

Slave Resistance

For most of the antebellum era, slaves made up one-third of the population of the Southern states. In some parts of the South, there were many more slaves than white people. South Carolina, for example, already had a slave majority in the 1700s. In the 1850s, sections of Mississippi had 20 slaves for every white resident.

Throughout the history of slavery in America, black people struggled to free themselves and control their own lives. Even though state laws made it difficult for them to resist, slaves rebelled on a day-to-day basis. They did this by running away, breaking tools, and otherwise undermining their masters' control. Slaves attempted larger rebellions as well, but these failed to secure their freedom and usually ended in the execution of the rebellions' leaders.

Most slave owners were ruthless in their pursuit of runaway slaves. These white men used dogs to hunt down a fugitive and trap him up a tree. Recaptured slaves were often brutally punished by whipping or torture.

Southern whites were always fearful of a possible slave uprising, especially in regions where they were outnumbered. They organized patrols to capture runaways and prevent slaves from plotting rebellions. Southern states also passed laws that ordered punishments for resistance to slavery. Aiding a runaway slave, for example, was punishable by whipping and fines as early as 1720 in South Carolina.

Despite these laws, Southern blacks organized three revolts in the United States. Two did not move far beyond the planning stages: Gabriel Prosser's Conspiracy in 1800 and the Denmark Vesey Conspiracy in 1822. In both cases, the planned rebellions were stopped just before they took place. In the aftermath of both plots, Southern planters brutally punished the conspirators and dozens of other slaves. They also restricted the movement of the South's free blacks, and tightened their control over the slave community.

Nat Turner's Rebellion

The most important slave revolt in the American South took place in Southampton County, Virginia. In 1831, Nat Turner and some 70 other slaves fought for their freedom. With pickaxes as their weapons, they hoped to seize the local armory and obtain their freedom by force. On August 21, Turner and five other slaves started a series of assaults on the county's plantations. By the next day, at least 60 slaves had joined in the attack and more than 50 white Southerners lay dead.

Turner's rebellion, however, did not result in freedom for any slaves. A couple of days after it began, soldiers put down the rebellion and executed the participants. White citizens also responded, but in less official ways. Across the region, masters punished slaves for their suspected participation. In all, white Virginians killed more than 100 blacks, and whipped and punished countless others.

Following Nat Turner's Rebellion, some Southern states were not sure how to handle the situation. The Virginia legislature held debates, and considered a bill to abolish, or end, slavery. The bill was narrowly defeated by 67 votes to 60.

"All my time, not devoted to my master's service, was spent either in prayer, or in making experiments in casting different things in moulds made of earth, in attempting to make paper, gun-powder, and many other experiments."

"Confession of Nat Turner," 1831

Virginia chose instead to place even tighter controls over slaves. They limited slaves' rights to move around the countryside, to be educated, and even to attend church. Virginia also made it harder for slaves to obtain their freedom and placed even stricter controls on the state's free blacks. Other Southern states responded with similar restrictions.

The Abolitionist Movement

While many white Southerners increased their dependence on slavery, many white Northerners began to question the institution of slavery for the first time. A few abolitionists— people who opposed slavery—had begun their crusade in the early 1700s. These early efforts resulted in legal restrictions on slavery in several colonies. In 1808, abolitionists cheered the end to the United States' participation in the trans-Atlantic slave trade. This meant that no more slaves could be imported into the United States. But they could still be sold within the nation itself.

Abolitionists turned their attention from the slave trade to the institution of slavery. Many of them wanted to end slavery altogether, but worried about the prospect of a large, free, black population in the United States. These early antislavery thinkers linked the freeing of slaves with their removal from the United States. This movement became known as "colonization." Most supporters of colonization thought that freed slaves should be taken to West Africa, while others suggested Haiti and Mexico.

The colonization movement lasted from about 1817 to 1830, but failed to gain long-term support. Other approaches to slavery became more prominent. In the 1820s, most abolitionists confined their efforts to printing pamphlets and delivering lectures. They declared that slavery was immoral and even unprofitable, and that "eventually" slavery should

After the 1831 slave uprising organized by Nat Turner, the leader of the rebellion, seen here, was tracked down and then executed. Nat Turner's Rebellion had severe consequences for other slaves in Virginia, many of whom were punished by their owners even though they had not taken part.

Colonization

The American Colonization Society was formed in 1817, shortly after Paul Cuffee attempted to settle freed slaves in Sierra Leone in West Africa. Cuffee was a wealthy black sea captain and whaling merchant from New Bedford, Massachusetts. He believed that blacks would have better opportunities in Sierra Leone than in the North of the United States.

Colonization offered a moderate position on the issue of slavery. It neither challenged the legality of slavery, nor did it declare the necessity of ending slavery. This idea at first appealed to some slave owners. It gave them a chance to continue owning slaves and to avoid living alongside a large population of free blacks. The state legislatures of Georgia, Virginia, Kentucky, Maryland, and Tennessee supported the early activities of the American Colonization Society. In 1832, nearly 70 percent of all the colonization societies were in the South.

In 1822, with the support of the American Colonization Society, a colony of freed American blacks was established in West Africa. This later became the nation of Liberia. Colonization societies founded several similar communities in West Africa, and about 15,000 freed African Americans settled in these colonies.

Colonization was not popular with many African Americans, however. Slaves wanted their freedom, but without leaving the United States. After generations of toiling on Southern fields, some slaves wanted to enjoy the benefits of their labor. And moving to Africa meant leaving friends and family behind in America. Other blacks felt that supporters of colonization were too quick to deny the possibility of a racially equal society. They would rather fight for their equality as free blacks within the United States.

By 1831, colonization had also fallen out of favor with slave owners. This change came about as Southerners began to defend slavery on moral grounds, saying that slaves needed the protection and guidance of white masters to prosper. Without the support of Southern slave owners or African Americans, the colonization movement slowed down considerably. Although Liberia remained a haven for African Americans, few American slaves found their way there after the 1820s.

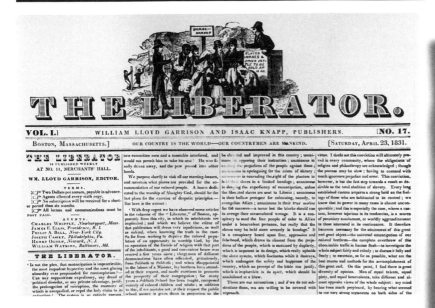

The abolitionist movement found a powerful voice in the words of the Liberator. *Founded in 1831 by William Lloyd Garrison, the newspaper campaigned tirelessly for the rights of black people until 1866, after the end of the Civil War.*

be "gradually" eliminated. These messages were designed to convince Southerners to abandon slavery, but the early abolitionists were often ignored. They were even harassed by their unsympathetic Northern neighbors. Abolitionists became more vocal in the 1830s, as part of a more general movement of social reform and religious revival. The American Antislavery Society was formed at the end of 1833 from three smaller abolitionist groups. One of its leaders was the newspaper publisher William Lloyd Garrison.

Garrison's early support came mostly from free blacks, who appreciated his stand against colonization and his calls for immediate abolition. Many of these black abolitionists were former slaves. Their firsthand knowledge of slavery, in addition to their well-spoken and civil behavior, aroused the sympathy of Northern audiences.

Former slaves lectured throughout the North and wrote books and essays about their experiences. Two of the most famous Southern slave memoirs were *Narrative of the Life of*

"Wo, wo, will be to you if we have to obtain our freedom by fighting. Throw way your fears and prejudices then, and enlighten us and treat us like men, and we will like you more than we do now hate you, an' tell us now no more about colonization, for America is as much our country, as it is yours."

David Walker, a free black in Boston, "An Appeal to the Colored Citizens of the World," 1829

"I will be as harsh as truth and as uncompromising as justice. On this subject [slavery], I do not wish to think, or speak, or write, with moderation. No! No!"

William Lloyd Garrison, first issue of the Liberator, *1831*

35

William Lloyd Garrison (1805–79)

William Garrison was born in Massachusetts and began learning the newspaper trade as a boy. In 1831, he started *The Liberator*, the most famous of abolitionist papers. He continued publishing the newspaper for the next 35 years. Garrison also began the New England Antislavery Society in 1832 and helped found the American Antislavery Society in 1833.

Garrison wanted immediate and total abolition, and wrote a constant stream of articles in *The Liberator* to demand this. Any compromise with slavery, he stated, was a compromise with sin. In addition, he was also against war, and so he refused to support the use of force. Southerners would have to be convinced through laws and words to rid their society of slavery.

Garrison had only a small personal following because of his extreme views. For instance, he wanted the North to secede from the Union because of the Constitution's proslavery provisions. He also opposed the Civil War until President Abraham Lincoln issued the Emancipation Proclamation in 1863.

Southerners saw abolitionists like Garrison as a real threat to their way of life. The Georgia legislature even offered $5,000 to anyone who could capture Garrison and bring him south to stand trial for "inciting rebellion."

Frederick Douglass and Harriet Jacobs's *Incidents in the Life of a Slave Girl, Written by Herself*. Jacobs's description of slavery was so well-written that many Americans refused to believe that it was written by either a woman or a former slave. Sojourner Truth was another former slave who campaigned on behalf of those still held captive.

For many years, abolitionism failed in its main purpose to rid the entire United States of slavery. But abolitionist speakers and authors kept the issues before the public and helped turn antislavery into a powerful political issue. By the 1830s, the abolitionist movement had united some blacks and whites in a common cause, and it continually gained strength.

Division in the Antislavery Movement

Many women supported the American Antislavery Society. Some of the most prominent were Helen E. Garrison, Lydia

Maria Child, and Maria W. Chapman. The participation of women in the abolitionist movement, however, was not always welcome. Some abolitionists believed that women should participate only in private, or play a lesser role.

In 1840, one group within the American Antislavery Society broke away to form a new organization, called the American and Foreign Antislavery Society. Its leaders were the long-time abolitionist Theodore Weld and the Southerners Angelina Grimké (Weld's wife) and Sarah Grimké.

Some antislavery people felt that abolitionists like Garrison went too far. They established the Liberty party, which aimed to oppose slavery more moderately and to campaign from within national government. This party, which was short-lived, nominated James G. Birney for president in 1840. The Liberty party never campaigned for the outright abolition of slavery, but instead fought to keep slaves out of the United States' Western territories. If the growth of slavery could be prevented, the supporters of the Liberty party thought that slavery would soon disappear.

This meeting on Boston Common was one of many where white people in the North got together to support the cause of abolishing slavery. Slowly, white Northerners began to free their slaves. But resistance to abolition only grew more fierce in the South.

37

Elijah Lovejoy was an abolitionist living in Alton, Illinois, where he published an antislavery newspaper, the Observer. *On November 7, 1837, his offices were beseiged by a proslavery mob that shot and killed Lovejoy when he tried to protect his printing presses from destruction.*

Opposition to Abolition

Even at its height, the antislavery movement never represented most Northerners. Throughout the nation, abolitionists faced resistance. Southerners outlawed all antislavery literature and banned abolitionists from their towns. Abolitionists faced opposition in the North, too. In New York City, angry crowds attacked abolitionist meetings in 1833. The next year, they attacked the American Antislavery Society's Fourth of July celebration. Nationwide, proslavery mobs injured and killed several abolitionists.

The opponents of abolitionism in the North had many motives. Some feared that the fight over slavery would result in a costly and destructive war. Others were afraid that the emancipation of slaves would result in a large, free, black population in the North. Still others, especially those involved in the textile industry, believed that slave labor was necessary to the nation's financial wellbeing.

Abolitionists were also resisted by Congress, where Southern representatives made it difficult for them to be heard. In 1836, abolitionists sent so many antislavery petitions to Congress that the House of Representatives passed a "gag rule," which automatically dismissed all of them. This meant that the petitions were not published for members to read, and Congress took no action on them.

The *Amistad*

In 1808, the United States stopped participating in the trans-Atlantic slave trade. Most nations had already done the same or would soon do so. Nevertheless, slave traders continued illegally to capture slaves in Africa.

In 1839, the Spanish ship *Amistad* carried 53 illegally-purchased slaves across the Atlantic Ocean. The captain of the *Amistad* defied Spanish law by smuggling the slaves from Sierra Leone, Africa, to Cuba. While the *Amistad* was moving the slaves from one Cuban port to another, the slaves rebelled. Their leader, named Cinque, escaped from his chains and released the other slaves. They killed the captain and ordered the ship's owners to sail back to Africa. Instead, the owners sailed northward until they were stopped by an American ship off Long Island, New York. The United States Coast Guard seized the *Amistad* and the Africans were taken to a jail in New Haven, Connecticut.

An argument over the slaves followed. Spain wanted the slaves returned to their Spanish owners, and United States President Martin Van Buren agreed. Abolitionists, however, protested. A court hearing in Hartford, Connecticut, determined that the slaves had not been legally enslaved and thus should be considered free. The Spanish government then appealed to the United States Supreme Court. Even though five of the nine Supreme Court justices were slave owners, the Court decided that the Africans were free. They were released and returned to their homeland.

The *Amistad* case was mostly forgotten for more than a century. Now it is remembered with a trail marking the story's main locations in Connecticut, and a monument at the site of the New Haven jail. The story of the *Amistad* became well-known when a movie on the subject was released in 1997.

Captured Africans aboard the Amistad *attack the crew and kill the ship's captain.*

4

Expansion and Compromise

I n the early 1800s, large numbers of Americans began to settle the lands between the Appalachian Mountains and the Mississippi River. Soon after, in 1819, the United States also acquired Florida from Spain. The future of the United States lay in expansion, but Northerners and Southerners disagreed about what that future would look like. At the heart of this disagreement was the issue of slavery and its future. Would the settlement of the West mean an expansion of Northern industry, or would it mean an expansion of Southern agriculture and slavery? As the nation extended its southern and western borders, tensions between the North and the South, or sectionalism, grew.

Florida

Even before Spain sold Florida to the United States, many Southerners wanted to move into the Spanish territory of Florida and onto the Indian lands east of the Mississippi River. The Spanish hold over Florida troubled both Southerners and Northerners. Not only did a foreign nation control the southeastern corner of the continent, but Americans were troubled by the Seminole Indians who lived in Florida. These Indian groups occasionally raided settlements in Georgia. The Seminoles also welcomed hundreds of fugitive African American slaves into their villages and the surrounding swamps.

In 1817, the United States Army invaded Florida in the hope of subduing the Seminoles and returning the fugitive slaves to their American owners. This task was more difficult

"So far from complying with the . . . treaty, [the Americans] are making daily encroachments and forging treaties (which they pretend are concluded with our people) for cessions and grants of land which were never in existence."

Seminole Chief Bowlegs to the governor of East Florida, 1816

40

Seminoles and Blacks in Florida

During the nineteenth century, southeastern Indian peoples began to use black slaves in ways similar to their white neighbors. The Seminole Indians of Florida were an exception to this. Rather than enslaving blacks, the Seminoles welcomed the newcomers as equals, taking them into their communities and sometimes even their families.

This began as early as 1770, and continued for the next 60 years. Fugitive slaves entered Indian villages, intermarried, and became black Seminoles. Other slaves formed separate communities within the swamps of Florida. These communities, called "negro towns" by American officials, had their own town leaders but pledged loyalty to the Seminole chiefs.

Seminole chief Osceola is captured by United States soldiers in the Second Seminole War.

Fugitive slaves and their descendants influenced Seminole culture and society. They frequently served as interpreters, were active in the deerskin trade, and became prominent political leaders and warriors. African Americans also fought alongside the Indians when they tried to resist removal in the Second Seminole War of the 1830s and 1840s.

than imagined. The Seminoles took advantage of their knowledge of the Florida swamps and avoided direct assaults by the Americans. Instead of giving way, the Seminoles attacked American soldiers in many small conflicts, causing frustration to American officials.

The Seminole Wars

After a series of annoying defeats by the Indians, the United States called upon Andrew Jackson, hero of the War of 1812, to stop Seminole raids into southern Georgia. Jackson, working under orders from Secretary of War John Calhoun,

In 1818, Andrew Jackson left Georgia with 1,000 men to invade Florida. Officially, he went to subdue the Seminole Indians, but in fact also waged a war against the Spanish who ruled the region. Jackson, seen here with his troops at Pensacola, took control of both Seminole strongholds and Spanish forts.

invaded Florida in 1818. Jackson was determined to punish the Seminoles for harboring escaped slaves. His actions began the conflict that is known as the First Seminole War.

When Jackson found fugitive slaves hiding near Fort Marks, he captured the Spanish outpost. The town of Pensacola, in the Florida panhandle, also fell into Jackson's hands. Jackson captured two British subjects, Alexander Arbuthnot and Robert Ambister, accused them of helping the Seminoles, and then executed them. However, he had not defeated the Seminoles, and runaway slaves continued to find refuge among the Indians. It took a Second Seminole War in the late 1830s and early 1840s, when Jackson himself was president, finally to defeat some Seminole groups and drive others deep into the Florida swamps.

Jackson's actions in 1818 were highly illegal. They were condemned by Congress, and the United States gave back to Spain the land Jackson had captured. Still, Jackson's "success" was very popular with many Americans, and his deeds were widely considered to be patriotic and courageous.

Jackson's capture of Florida strengthened the United States' position with Spain. President James Monroe now told Spain that it had no choice but to let Florida become part of the United States. If Spain refused, the United States would make Florida its protectorate, which meant American troops would be stationed there to weaken Spanish control. So, in the Adams-Onís Treaty of 1819, Spain gave all of Florida to the United States. In return, the United States took responsibility for nearly $5 million in debts that American merchants claimed from Spain. The treaty also settled the western boundary of the Louisiana Territory and gave the United States a claim to Spanish Texas.

Andrew Jackson (1767–1845)

Andrew Jackson was born to a poor family in the Carolina backcountry. During the American Revolution, he was captured by the British and placed in prison. His family was not so lucky. All but one of his immediate relatives died during the war.

When the war ended, Jackson moved west and studied law. He began work as a prosecuting attorney in what is now Tennessee. Jackson was elected to Congress and then the Senate, and later joined the Tennessee Supreme Court. He also became a wealthy plantation owner.

Jackson joined the military and, during the War of 1812, helped defeat the Creek Indians in what is now Alabama and beat the British at the Battle of New Orleans. In 1818, Jackson furthered his military reputation by fighting the Seminoles and capturing Florida.

Later, Jackson returned to politics and ran for the presidency in 1824. He lost that election, but won the presidency in 1828. As president, Jackson tried to fight any federal policy that seemed to support wealthy Americans at the expense of the common man. He attempted to limit the powers of federal government. He also tried to destroy the Second Bank of the United States, which was believed to serve the interests of the rich rather than the poor. This added to his reputation as the protector of working people.

After a second term as president, Jackson returned to his home in Nashville, where he lived until his death.

Expansion onto Indian Lands

At the same time that Florida became American territory, Southerners were spreading into Indian territory in other parts of the South. They moved into areas that are now parts of Georgia, Alabama, Mississippi, South Carolina, North Carolina, Kentucky, Tennessee, and Louisiana. State governments and the United States government imposed many treaties onto local tribes, and Indians were forced to sell much of their land. In return for their lands in the East, the Indians were promised money, lands in the West, and an end to the constant invasion of white settlers. In the early 1800s, Creek, Cherokee, Chickasaw, and Choctaw peoples all ceded some of their eastern lands to the United States. Some Indians left or were removed to areas set aside as Indian Territory, settling mainly in what is now Oklahoma.

The lands acquired from the Indians in the South were often perfectly suited to large-scale cotton farming. Southern planters and their slaves moved in. By 1820, the plantation system in the South extended to both sides of the Mississippi River.

Northerners and Southerners Move West

To the north of this southernmost region, people from the East began to move west along four main routes. Those from the South moved into the areas south of the Ohio River along the Cumberland Road from Maryland to the Ohio River in Virginia (now West Virginia). Or they followed the Wilderness Road, from Virginia through the Cumberland Gap into Kentucky. Some Northerners followed the Lancaster Turnpike from Philadelphia to Pittsburgh. Others moved along the Genesee Road, from Albany, New York, to Buffalo, New York, on Lake Erie. (See map on page 18.)

A Conestoga wagon heads west along the busy Cumberland Road. The turnpike eventually became part of the National Road, which stretched all the way from Cumberland, Maryland, to Vandalia, Illinois.

Northerners moving into the Great Lakes area settled in and around hundreds of small new towns. They built houses, cleared land for crops, and grew corn. But nowhere was westward expansion more welcome than in the agricultural South. Its earliest agricultural lands along the Atlantic coast were worn out after 200 years of farming, and the old tobacco and cotton fields were producing smaller and smaller crops. Western lands gave Southern planters new, fertile farmland and increased their acreage. Settlement in both regions of the West brought an increase in prosperity for farms and for the nation as a whole.

An Uneasy Balance

Northerners and Southerners carried their sectional attitudes with them as they moved westward. The northern section of the West, or the Northwest, was mostly opposed to an extension of slavery. The southern section of the West, or the Southwest, favored slavery. Rather than allowing the West to emerge as a third region, the expansion of white settlement simply enabled the Northern and Southern societies to extend west. This led to increasing sectional debates in the country and in Congress.

In 1819, the United States had a political balance. There were 22 states in the Union. 11 Southern states had slavery and 11 Northern states had done away with slavery or were freeing their slaves gradually. This balance had its benefits, as it meant neither North nor South controlled the nation's lawmaking. It also let the nation put off a final decision on how it would handle the issue of slavery.

However, as Americans organized the Western territories and prepared to admit them into the Union as states, this balance was no longer secure. Would the new states be slave states or free states? Would the political balance between North and South, free and slave states, be maintained? Could compromises be found, or would conflict tear the regions apart?

Northerners and Southerners often feared the worst. Many Northerners were afraid that the balance would shift in the slave owners' direction and lead to new constitutional protections for slavery. Some worried that, soon, slavery would be legal in all of the states. Southerners, for their part, worried that the balance would shift in favor of the North and therefore result in slavery being unable to expand. Northern control of Congress, they believed, might even end slavery altogether.

The Debate about Missouri

In 1817, the territory of Missouri first threatened to upset the fragile balance. Missouri, a Western territory that allowed slavery, wanted to become a state. According to the existing laws for turning territories into states, Missouri's population had grown large enough to apply for statehood. It was up to Congress to make the rules that would let Missouri into the Union. Congress debated Missouri's statehood and what it would do to the political balance between North and South. Would western expansion of slavery make the South as rich and powerful as the North?

Northern states wanted to keep slavery from spreading to Missouri and any other new states. In 1819, Representative James Tallmadge of New York saw the Missouri question as an opportunity for the North to slow down the expansion of slavery. He suggested, in the Tallmadge Amendment, that the United States should only admit Missouri as a state if it stopped bringing in new slaves. He also said that children born there to enslaved parents should be freed when they reached the age of 25.

The Tallmadge Amendment echoed a policy of gradual emancipation that already existed in New York and other Northern states. Not surprisingly, Southerners strongly opposed this amendment. They wanted to keep the right to take their property, including slaves, anywhere in the United States. Senator Thomas W. Cobb of Georgia said that the Tallmadge Amendment lit "a fire which all the waters of the ocean cannot put out and which seas of blood can only extinguish."

"The President [James Monroe] thinks this question [the expansion of slavery] will be winked away by a compromise. But so do not I. Much am I mistaken if it is not destined to survive his political and individual life and mine."

John Quincy Adams, after the Missouri Compromise, 1820

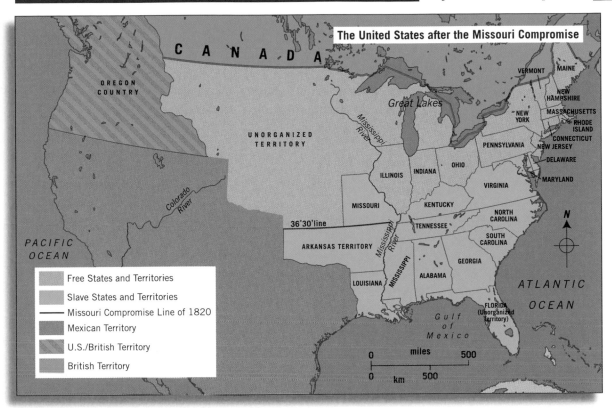

The United States after the Missouri Compromise

Free States and Territories
Slave States and Territories
Missouri Compromise Line of 1820
Mexican Territory
U.S./British Territory
British Territory

The Tallmadge Amendment passed in the House of Representatives but was defeated in the Senate. Northerners and Southerners in Congress could not agree on a policy, and Missouri remained a territory. The debate then became a public one. A few people in both the North and the South wanted their states to secede if Missouri's slavery position did not please them.

The Missouri Compromise

Congress finally decided the issue through a compromise, introduced by Representative Henry Clay of Kentucky. For the Northerners, Clay suggested slavery should be kept out of all western lands north of the 36°30' latitude line. This was the Arkansas-Missouri boundary. To please Southerners, the compromise made Missouri an exception to this rule. Missouri could keep its slaves, but it had to allow free African Americans to move west and settle there.

This map shows how the United States and U.S. territories were divided into those that allowed slavery and those in which slavery was banned. The Missouri Compromise kept the balance by admitting Maine as a free state and Missouri as a slave state.

To keep an equal number of slave and free states, Maine (until then a part of Massachusetts) was admitted to the Union without slavery. It would become the twelfth free state and Missouri would be the twelfth slave state. The Missouri Compromise stayed in effect until 1854, but the issue of slavery's expansion continued to divide the nation. Thomas Jefferson, the former United States president, said the Missouri Compromise "like a fire-bell in the night, awakened and filled me with terror."

Emancipation

The strategy of giving slaves their freedom slowly, or gradual emancipation, was well known throughout the North in the antebellum period. In fact, because emancipation was introduced gradually in the North, more than 16 percent of Northern blacks were still slaves in 1819.

Before the American Revolution, all 13 American colonies had slavery. But during the war for independence, some Americans recognized the contradiction between owning slaves and the principles of equality they claimed for their new nation in the Declaration of Independence. Many Northerners considered immediately ending slavery, but slave owners pushed for the alternative of gradual emancipation. This gave liberty to slaves, but also protected slave owners' rights in the short term. Only Massachusetts and Vermont gave slaves immediate freedom.

Most Southern slaves did not receive their freedom until the Civil War ended in 1865. Even after the Civil War, freedom in both North and South was not followed by racial equality. Instead, free blacks faced prejudice and limited rights that continued into the twentieth century. Only from the second half of the twentieth century were African Americans guaranteed equality under American law. Civil rights protesters in the 1950s and 1960s secured an end to legal segregation. But even today, African Americans are still fighting for racial equality.

5

Disputes Divide the Nation

T he "Era of Good Feelings," which began with Monroe's presidency in 1816, faded quickly in the face of growing disputes within the United States. However, it left its mark in a new attitude to foreign policy.

The Monroe Doctrine

The United States had built up its army and navy during the War of 1812. When the war ended, the armed forces remained strong, and the nation took pride in its new military powers. America was determined to protect its expanding territory and its interests abroad. In 1823, President Monroe made a declaration to the rest of the world that reflected this. His policy became known as the Monroe Doctrine.

The Monroe Doctrine had three major points. First, it declared that European powers could no longer view the Americas as future colonial territory. Second, it stated that any attempts by European nations to expand their type of

This cartoon from the New York Herald *in the late 1800s shows European leaders facing the Monroe Doctrine and the military might of the United States, represented here by two battleships. The Doctrine continued to influence U.S. foreign policy and relations with the rest of the world into the twentieth century.*

James Monroe (1758–1831)

James Monroe was born in Virginia. After fighting in the Revolutionary War, he studied law alongside his classmate Thomas Jefferson. He served in the Virginia legislature and the Continental Congress, and then became governor of Virginia.

Monroe was a diplomat in France while Jefferson was president of the United States. When Jefferson told him to buy New Orleans, Monroe instead arranged the purchase of the entire Louisiana region in 1803. The Louisiana Purchase doubled the size of the United States.

When James Madison was president, Monroe served as secretary of state and then as secretary of war. Monroe himself became the fifth president of the United States in 1816 and was reelected in 1820.

Today, Monroe is best known for issuing the Monroe Doctrine which declared that the United States would not interfere in Europe. Nor would it allow Europeans to interfere in America. The doctrine let the world know that the United States planned to be the main military power in the Americas. Monroe was also active in the colonization movement to remove freed slaves to Africa, and Monrovia, the capital of Liberia, is named for him.

"The American continents, by the free and independent condition which they have assumed and maintain, are henceforth not to be considered as subjects for future colonization by any European powers."

President James Monroe, Annual Message to Congress, 1823

political system in the Americas would be seen as a threat to the United States. Third, it asserted that the United States would not interfere with existing European colonial arrangements in the Americas, would not get involved in European affairs, and would not take part in European foreign wars.

Tariffs and the American System

Meanwhile, sectional disputes within Congress grew. Many political debates centered around the difficult topic of tariffs, or taxes on imported goods. Northern industrialists and Southern planters disagreed over what type of tariff would be good for the United States. Textile manufacturers in the North thought that their growing industries needed a high tariff to protect them from competing European textile mills. Most Southerners, on the other hand, wanted low tariffs.

This was because the region imported many items from overseas and low tariffs allowed Southerners to buy foreign goods cheaply.

In 1816, to the outrage of Southerners, Congress passed a high tariff. For Northern industry, the high tariff enabled great economic growth. In the South, it resulted in an economic downturn.

Henry Clay, who had brought about the Missouri Compromise, believed that the industrial North and agricultural South could resolve their differences and thereby save their economies. Both regions had economic needs, and Congress had to assure both Northerners and Southerners that their interests would be preserved. In 1824, Clay proposed an economic compromise that he called the "American System."

Clay's "American System" offered both regions something they wanted. To protect Northern manufacturing from foreign competition, Clay's system recommended continuing the high tariff. In return, Clay offered something equally important to the South, which opposed high tariffs. Slavery, Clay declared, could continue in both old and new states. Furthermore, all Americans would benefit from the nation's financial support for a wide range of internal improvements. The federal government would pay to improve and expand the nation's roads and waterways.

The American System nearly gained the support of Congress. The major problem was that many members of Congress did not believe that, under the Constitution, the federal government was allowed to pay for internal improvements. The vote in the House of Representatives went according to sectional interests. New England and the Southeastern states opposed it. Other Northern and Western states favored it.

Henry Clay was the mastermind behind many important government plans in the first half of the 1800s. After forging the Missouri Compromise of 1821, he proposed the American System to solve the dispute over tariffs. The plan was not adopted, but Clay continued to try and resolve differences between North and South throughout his political career.

The Disputed Election of 1824

In the 1820s, political parties selected their presidential candidates through informal groups of congressmen called caucuses. In 1824, the Republican caucus nominated William Crawford from Georgia. This decision was widely unpopular. Crawford had few supporters outside of Congress and support for him dropped further when he suffered a disabling stroke in the summer of 1824.

Several states nominated three other candidates: John Quincy Adams from Massachusetts, Andrew Jackson from Tennessee, and Henry Clay from Kentucky. John Quincy Adams was the son of the second president, John Adams, and had served in government as a senator, diplomat, and secretary of state. He was known for his intelligence and political skills. Jackson, a slave owner from Tennessee and war hero, ran for office without much of a political record.

Jackson received the most electoral votes in the 1824 election, but he did not win a majority of all the votes cast. For the first time, therefore, the final vote for president had to be made in the House of Representatives.

The Twelfth Amendment to the Constitution stated that the House could only consider the top three vote-winners: Jackson, Adams, and Crawford. Clay had to drop out of the race. He then gave his support to Adams and convinced other congressmen to do the same. Adams became president, and he immediately named Clay as his secretary of state.

Jackson's supporters were furious that the House did not choose the candidate with the most votes. Adams's election was a "corrupt bargain," they said, and Congress "stole" Jackson's victory. Still, Jackson maintained the loyalty of his supporters and was certain to be nominated again in 1828.

President Adams's Style

Adams was deliberately nonpolitical in his governing style. For example, he did not fire good staff members just because their political beliefs differed from his own. He also stretched his presidential powers to recommend a series of programs

John Quincy Adams (1767–1848)

John Quincy Adams was born in Braintree, Massachusetts. He was the eldest son of John Adams, the second president of the United States. The younger Adams is often named as the most intelligent of U.S. presidents even though he was not a very successful one.

Adams was elected to the Senate as a member of the Federalist party in 1802. He resigned before his term ended, however, and soon after was appointed to the first in a series of diplomatic posts. He later led the peace negotiations with Britain at the end of the War of 1812. Adams served in a number of other capacities before he became secretary of state to President Monroe. In this position, Adams was responsible for writing the Monroe Doctrine, and for acquiring Florida from Spain.

In 1824, Adams won the presidency but only served one term. He lost the election of 1828 to Andrew Jackson. In 1831, Adams was elected to the House of Representatives, where he fought for the right of antislavery groups to present their views to Congress. In 1839, Adams successfully defended the 53 Africans from the slave ship *Amistad* in their case before the Supreme Court.

that he hoped would make the United States a leader in technology. Adams wanted the government to promote the arts and sciences in addition to agriculture, manufacturing, and business. He proposed establishing an astronomical observatory and a national university. Like most people, Adams wanted the nation to build more roads and canals.

However, most Southern politicians disagreed with Adams's programs because they involved giving even more power to the federal government. Southerners wanted internal improvements, but did not believe that the federal government should pay for them. That responsibility, they felt, belonged to the states and private individuals. Vice President John Calhoun protected the interest of his fellow Southerners by opposing the president's plans. Most of Adams's program never became law.

Meanwhile, Jackson's movement for popular democracy, or giving more power to the common people, continued to grow. Women and black people were not allowed to vote, but new state constitutions in Alabama, Illinois, Indiana, and Maine between 1816 and 1820 gave the vote to all white males. Previously, men's right to vote had depended on property ownership and paying taxes. Between 1818 and 1821, New York, Connecticut, and Massachusetts also let more white men vote by abolishing the requirement to own property.

Jackson Becomes President

Jackson's popularity and the changes in voting laws helped him in the 1828 presidential election. After the Tennessee state legislature nominated him for president, Jackson campaigned for the "democracy of numbers" and against the "moneyed aristocracy." This time, he won the election. It was more of a people's victory than any other had been. Jackson received 1.1 million votes, and more than half of all eligible voters went to vote in the elections. Four years earlier, only one in four eligible voters had done so.

Jackson was the first president from a state other than Virginia or Massachusetts. Unlike Adams, he was intensely political and intended to be a powerful president. Jackson trusted his feelings more than he listened to trained experts. He rewarded his political supporters with well-paying government jobs, even if they were not qualified for them. This was widely known as the "spoils system." Jackson also had a group of people he trusted who acted as his unofficial advisors. Many of them were personal friends, not professional Washington politicians, and they often had little experience in government.

This election poster from Andrew Jackson's 1828 presidential campaign of presents "Old Hickory," as he was known, as a man of honesty and a man of the people. It refers also to the earlier election of John Quincy Adams in 1824. Jackson's supporters claimed that Adams had beaten Jackson because of a "corrupt bargain" with Henry Clay, who had been appointed secretary of state in exchange for his support of Adams.

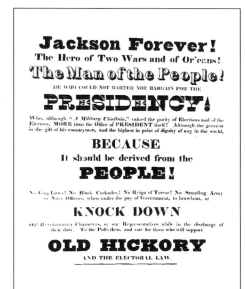

54

When Jackson was elected, he said his presidency would be based on supporting states' rights, improving the civil service, and fighting the interests of the rich. In other words, Jackson wanted the government to be on the side of "the people." States' rights meant that the federal government would leave many decisions and powers in the hands of individual states. Jackson's improvement of the civil service meant that he would try to make government workers and services more efficient.

Jackson hoped as well to expand the powers of the presidency. This brought him into conflict with another strong figure who had held office in Washington for decades: Supreme Court Chief Justice John Marshall. During Jackson's presidency, these two men clashed several times.

Since 1801, Marshall had fought to expand the federal government's power by using the Constitution's "implied powers" clause. This meant that the federal government had any power that the Constitution did not specifically give to the states. Marshall also strengthened the Supreme Court by giving it the power of judicial review. This power allows the Supreme Court to review rulings made in lower courts and laws made by Congress, and to decide whether or not they are constitutional. These powers directly opposed the states' rights idea, which Jackson supported.

This cartoon of 1829 is entitled "The President's Levée [reception], or All Creation Going to the White House." It was intended to make fun of the scene at Jackson's inauguration, when an unruly crowd of supporters entered the usually dignified White House.

Moving the Indians West

President Jackson also declared he would have a "just and liberal policy" toward Indians. In practice, however, this meant moving the Indians from their traditional homelands and onto reservations (areas of land set aside for Indians) west of the Mississippi River. This policy resulted in one of Jackson's many conflicts with Marshall.

"We are aware that some persons suppose it will be for our advantage to remove beyond the Mississippi. We think otherwise. Our people universally think otherwise. . . . We cannot endure to be deprived of our national and individual rights and subjected to a process of intolerable oppression."

"Memorial of the Cherokee Nation," 1830

The Indian Removal Act

In the early nineteenth century, tens of thousands of Native Americans from the Southeast endured removal from their homelands. Indian removal was an official United States policy. Although some Americans protested that it was cruel and illegal, most favored Indian removal. In May 1830, Congress passed the Indian Removal Act. This law authorized President Jackson to negotiate removal treaties with some of the Indian peoples—Choctaws, Chickasaws, Creeks, Cherokees, and Seminoles—living east of the Mississippi River.

The Choctaws, whose homelands were in Alabama and Mississippi, were the first to face removal, in 1830. Over the next three years, the Choctaws left their homelands to move west into Indian Territory. Their journey was described by the French historian Alexis de Tocqueville as a "sight [that] will never fade from my memory."

The Cherokee Indians, mostly living in Georgia, attempted to keep their homelands by taking legal action. Their legal victories, however, were no help to them and in 1838, the United States army moved in. The Cherokees were confined to disease-ridden removal camps in their homelands for several months before the federal troops pushed them west.

The journeys were usually taken on foot, and the United States rarely met its promises to provide food and medical supplies. Thousands of Native Americans, including one-quarter of the Cherokees, lost their lives on what is called the "Trail of Tears." Those who survived ended their journey in present-day Oklahoma, hundreds of miles from their homelands. By 1840, nearly all of the Southeastern Indians had died or were living west of the Mississippi River.

The Cherokees were the largest Indian group to face Jackson's policy of Indian removal. Their lands stretched from the Carolinas and Georgia into Tennessee, Alabama, and Mississippi. The Cherokees tried to resist Jackson's plans. In two court cases, the Supreme Court confirmed the independence of the Cherokee Nation from either state or federal control. When Justice Marshall announced this, Jackson supposedly said, "John Marshall has made his decision, now let him enforce it!" In spite of its ruling, the Supreme Court had no means to prevent Jackson or individual states from removing Indians. By 1838, the U.S. military had forced most Cherokees into Indian Territory, a large reservation in what is now Oklahoma.

The Tariff and Nullification

The struggle over the tariff returned during Andrew Jackson's presidency and showed how serious the sectional divide had become. The federal tariff was raised again in 1828, to the dismay of many Southerners. They felt that the Tariff of 1828, which they called the "Tariff of Abominations," was the final blow to their region's economy. One Alabama politician declared that the tariff was "little less than legalized [theft]." Many Southerners were angry enough to discuss seceding from the United States.

Vice President Calhoun had a different idea. Rather than leaving the Union, Calhoun believed that the Southern states should simply veto, or nullify, the federal law. Calhoun decided that the Constitution gave the states this power of nullification. The Senate debated nullification in early 1830. As vice president, Calhoun could not take part in the debate. Senator Robert Hayne of South Carolina took his place in explaining that nullification was allowed under United States law. He was opposed by Senator Daniel

John Calhoun was vice president under Andrew Jackson during the nullification crisis of the 1830s. He believed that the states had the right to veto federal laws. In 1832, his difference with President Jackson over states' rights caused Calhoun to resign as vice president.

"Our Union. Next to our liberty, most dear. May we all remember that it can only be preserved by respecting the rights of the States and by distributing equally the benefits and burdens of the Union."

Vice President John Calhoun, in a toast at Thomas Jefferson's birthday banquet, 1830

"To say that any state may at pleasure secede from the Union is to say that the United States is not a nation. . . . Disunion by armed force is treason. Are you really ready to incur its guilt? If you are, on the heads of the instigators of the act be the dreadful consequences."

President Andrew Jackson, Proclamation on Nullification to the People of South Carolina, 1832

Webster of Massachusetts, who declared that the Constitution and national government held supreme power over the states.

The issue of tariffs would not disappear. Congress passed a slightly lower tariff bill in 1832. Still, it was not low enough to please many Southerners, and a South Carolina convention passed a nullification bill late in 1832. This bill said South Carolina would not pay the federal tariff after February 1, 1833, and that the state would secede from the nation if the government used force to collect it. President Jackson responded to this threat by sending warships, troops, and guns to Charleston. He told South Carolina that the taxes would be collected and the Union maintained.

Both Clay and Calhoun feared the situation. Clay wanted to prevent Jackson from using the military to force South Carolina to pay the tariff. Calhoun was afraid that the United States was about to break up. Together, in 1833, they wrote a compromise called the Force Bill, which Congress passed. Under this law, Congress allowed the president to use troops to collect the taxes. At the same time, Congress passed a law lowering the tariff by 20 percent over the next ten years. This compromise ended the crisis.

The Bank of the United States

In 1832, Jackson clashed with other politicians, this time about the Bank of the United States. In 1816, Congress had founded the Second Bank of the United States to take care of the nation's financial affairs after the War of 1812. The bank held the federal government's funds and had branches throughout the nation.

The bank's policies were set in the Northeast, and Jackson thought they favored wealthy businesses and bankers over ordinary farmers. He believed most Americans, especially farmers and poor people in the West, were shut out of the banking system or were charged unfairly high rates of interest (the amount of extra money they had to pay back on loans from the bank). Henry Clay disagreed, and believed that the

Henry Clay (1777–1852) and John C. Calhoun (1782–1850)

Henry Clay and John Calhoun were two of the most important politicians in antebellum America. Clay worked to preserve national unity, while Calhoun tried to protect the interests of South Carolina and the South in general.

In an era of sectional conflict, Americans referred to Clay as the "Great Compromiser" and "Great Pacificator." During his long career in the House of Representatives, Clay drew up the Missouri Compromise. He became a senator in 1831, and was responsible for the tax compromise of 1833 and the Compromise of 1850. He also suggested the "American System" to keep North and South together. Clay was leader of the Whig party that formed in 1834. He made three unsuccessful runs for president in 1824, 1832, and 1844.

John Calhoun was known as the South's chief spokesperson during the antebellum era. Like Henry Clay, he had been a "war hawk," or a supporter of the War of 1812, because he believed that the war with Britain was good for the nation and for the South. In the years that followed, Calhoun served as James Monroe's secretary of war, and he was elected vice president under Presidents John Quincy Adams and Andrew Jackson.

Calhoun opposed the "Tariff of Abominations" of 1828. He responded to the tariff with the idea of states' rights. This theory declared that states were voluntary members of the Union and therefore could withdraw their support for federal laws if they chose to. The crisis ended in 1833 when Clay and Calhoun came up with a compromise that satisfied President Jackson and the South.

Calhoun continued to represent Southern interests after the nullification crisis. As secretary of state under President Tyler, Calhoun pushed Congress to approve the annexation of Texas. In his last Senate speech, he supported the Compromise of 1850, but said it did not provide enough support for states' rights.

Bank of the United States was essential to the nation's prosperity. Clay fought to save the bank, and this created a showdown between Jackson and the bank's supporters.

Congress voted to keep the bank going, but Jackson immediately vetoed this. The president declared that the Bank of the United States was not mentioned in the

Constitution, that it was a monopoly controlled by eastern bankers, and that it opposed the interests of small western banks. Jackson's attack on the bank did not end there. In 1833, he tried to destroy the "monster" bank by withdrawing all government funds from it and depositing the money in smaller state banks. The Bank of the United States struggled without the federal deposits, and the nation lost its national bank in 1836.

Jackson and his supporters saw the Bank of the United States as too powerful and as unfavorable to the interests of ordinary people. Jackson is seen here slaying the "many-headed monster," which he did by withdrawing the federal government's money from the bank.

The Whig Party Forms

In 1834, during Andrew Jackson's second term as president, Jackson's opponents formed a political party known as the Whigs. The name came from the British Whig party, which had supported the powers of the English government against the king in the 1600s. American Whigs favored expanding the power of Congress and wanted to encourage industrial and commercial growth. Whigs claimed that their policies would benefit all Americans, but they emphasized the importance of business and industry in creating economic growth.

The Whigs, led by Henry Clay, were mostly former National Republicans, a group that had split from the old Republican party. The new Whig party attracted members of the business community because it supported paying for internal improvements with government money, expanding trade, and a national bank.

The Whig party also attracted many members of smaller political parties who brought with them their own beliefs. One group was the Nativists, who feared the influence of immigrants. In addition, some Southern planters and supporters of states' rights joined the Whigs in protest at Jackson's opposition to nullification.

Perhaps the most important party that joined the Whigs was the Anti-Masonic party. It opposed Jackson because he was a member of the Freemasons. The Freemasons, a worldwide group, devoted themselves to vaguely religious rituals at their meetings and kept their actions hidden from the public. Their secrecy aroused the fears of outsiders.

In 1840, the Whig party had gathered enough supporters to elect William Henry Harrison as the nation's president. Harrison, an elderly hero of the Battle of Tippecanoe during the War of 1812, died after only a few months in office. Vice President John Tyler then became the nation's president.

States' Rights

When the Founding Fathers wrote the Constitution of the United States of America, they tried to establish the powers of individual states and the federal government. But the exact balance between states' rights and federal rights was unclear, and the issue was left up to future generations to decide.

The states' rights idea was first used in 1798 and 1799. Thomas Jefferson and James Madison argued that the powers of the states should be protected against new federal laws. They even declared the states had the right to nullify federal laws that were not mentioned in the Constitution. The idea reappeared in 1832 to 1833, when South Carolina tried to use states' rights to nullify the federal tariff. The state was unsuccessful.

Still, the idea of states' rights did not disappear. After Abraham Lincoln was elected president in 1860, Southern states declared that they had the right to leave or secede from the Union. Lincoln never accepted this theory. Even as the Civil War progressed, he treated the Confederate states as if they were just in a state of "rebellion" rather than a separate nation.

In 1948, some Southerners returned to states' rights to fight civil rights legislation. And in more recent years, many congressmen have called for returning power to the states. Issues ranging from gun control to deciding what is taught in public schools have attracted modern states' rights supporters.

6

Manifest Destiny

As the nation's eyes focused on western growth, the North and the South became more defensive of their opposing positions on slavery. Northerners pushed to end the expansion of slavery and limit the rights of slave owners. Southerners, for their part, were demanding protection of their rights, and an increase in power for the states.

Texas

Settlers from the United States began arriving in Texas in the 1820s. The area, previously under Spanish control, had recently become Mexican territory. The first Americans were led to Texas by Stephen Austin, a pioneer from Virginia. Austin convinced Mexico to allow the American immigrants to bring their slaves into the area. By 1835, over 30,000 black and white Americans had settled on what was Mexican land. The white settlers had no intention of becoming Mexicans. They wanted to continue to speak English and keep their American customs.

Most of the Americans in Texas came from Southern states. When the Mexican government abolished slavery in 1831, these Texans protested. Their rights as slave owners were being threatened. This led the Americans in Texas to declare their independence and legalize slavery in 1836.

The city of Austin in 1840, several years after American settlement began in Texas. The city was named for Stephen Austin who brought the first American settlers, or Anglos, to the region in the 1820s.

Texan Independence

In 1835, General Antonio López de Santa Anna seized control of Mexico and its territories, including Texas. He declared himself Mexico's leader and quickly increased the power of the nation's government. The American residents in Texas believed that this threatened their way of life and, in 1836, declared their independence.

General Sam Houston at the Battle of San Jacinto in 1836.

Mexico refused to recognize Texan independence, and Texan Americans there began to rebel against Mexican rule. President Santa Anna and his Mexican forces won the first battles with the Texans. The most famous of these battles occurred at the Alamo, a fortified former mission in San Antonio occupied by American rebels. On March 6, 1836, after 12 days under siege by Santa Anna's force of 3,000 Mexican soldiers, the Alamo fell to its attackers. All 187 of the American and Texan defenders inside the Alamo died.

In late April 1836, General Sam Houston and his rebel forces defeated the Mexicans at the Battle of San Jacinto. Their battle cry was "Remember the Alamo!" And with this victory, Texas won the right to be an independent republic. Stephen Austin, who had founded the first American colonies in Texas, was called the "Father of Texas" for his role in gaining independence. The head of the army, General Samuel Houston, became Texas's greatest hero.

The citizens of the new republic elected Houston as Texas's president, but soon applied to join the United States. It was several years before Texas became a state, in June 1845.

For ten years, Texas was an independent republic, or nation. During that decade it had three presidents (Sam Houston, Mirabeau Lamar, and Anson Jones) and its own constitution. Nevertheless, most Texans wanted to become part of the United States. Texas's future, however, was tied to the sectional disputes in nineteenth-century America. If Texas became a state, it would come with slavery. This would result in the nation having more proslavery states than antislavery states. Texas, therefore, threatened the sectional balance.

In 1838, Sam Houston asked the United States to annex Texas, but Congress turned him down. Northern Whigs feared that Texas would be divided into several proslavery states. This might give proslavery forces permanent control of the national government.

Texas's next president, Mirabeau Lamar, wanted Texas to stay independent. He faced the opposition of many Americans and Texans. The Mexican government also objected because it still had not recognized Texan independence. In 1843, Mexico's president, Antonio López de Santa Anna, announced that any annexation of Texas by the United States would be the same as a declaration of war. In 1844, supported by President Tyler, John Calhoun drew up an annexation treaty. But senators opposed to slavery turned down the treaty by a margin of two to one.

The future of Texas remained undecided as the 1844 presidential campaign approached. The question of Texas annexation would become one of the main election issues.

The 1844 election

The other major issue of the 1844 presidential campaign concerned Oregon. Unlike Texas, Oregon was settled by Americans from Northern states. The region was widely considered against slavery, and few Southerners had plans to move there with their slaves. The problem was that both the United States and Britain claimed "Oregon Country."

Americans who favored United States expansion connected the Texas and Oregon questions. If both territories became states, the balance between slave states and free states would continue. Texas would favor slavery, and Oregon would oppose it. For some parties, their presidential campaigns focused on this issue. The Democratic party (formerly the Democratic Republicans) nominated James K. Polk from

In 1843, white settlers met at Champoeg in the Oregon Territory to adopt a constitution for their territorial government. They also voted in support of United States rather than British rule. But the British were reluctant to give up their claim to the Columbia River area, and the boundary dispute in Oregon was not settled until 1846.

The Oregon Trail

In 1833, missionaries from the East began heading to Oregon, following a report that the Indians there were eager to become Christians. The report was untrue, but the missionaries found a region filled with fertile lands and natural beauty. Word spread, and Oregon became an opportunity for American expansion.

Thousands of white American settlers took the Oregon Trail west in the 1840s and 1850s. The overland route, originally used by a handful of fur traders and trappers, stretched from Independence, Missouri, to the Willamette Valley in Oregon. The trip took about six months.

The Oregon Trail cut right through the territory of the Plains Indians. The Sioux, Cheyenne, Apache, and Comanche peoples hunted buffalo for most of their needs. They feared the arrival of white Americans on their lands, and there was indeed much to fear. Americans brought to the region new diseases that infected and killed the Indians. They also killed the buffalo for sport, leaving thousands of the dead animals to rot. Although American settlers feared the Plains Indians, fewer than 400 of them were killed by Indians between 1840 and 1860. Many more Indians died at the hands of American troops and migrants on the Oregon Trail.

Settlers stopped using the trail in the 1870s, by which time the railroad was offering an easier and cheaper means of traveling west. By then, over 350,000 migrants had gone west along the Oregon Trail.

James Polk, eleventh president of the United States, believed strongly in American expansion. During his presidency, the Oregon question was settled, and California and the Southwest were won from Mexico.

Tennessee. Some Democrats disagreed with this choice and nominated President Tyler at a separate meeting. Both Polk and Tyler favored American expansion and slavery, but their rivalry split the Democratic vote.

Meanwhile, the Whigs nominated Henry Clay, who did not refer to the Texas issue. He supported the Whig policies of strengthening the powers of Congress and improving economic growth. Clay would have won the election, had a new political party not taken votes away from him. The Liberty party, formed by abolitionists in 1844, supported its founder, James Birney, in the election. Birney campaigned on the slavery issue and opposed expansion of slavery into the West. He won many votes away from Clay in New York. Polk managed to win the state and was elected president.

In his last act as president, Tyler successfully supported a resolution to annex Texas. Texas accepted the terms of the resolution and was admitted to the Union as a single state.

Manifest Destiny

Most Americans had long held the idea that their country would naturally expand across the continent. In 1846, this belief was given a name by John L. O'Sullivan, editor of the *United States Magazine and Democratic Review*. The United States should fulfill its "manifest destiny . . . allotted by Providence" to spread across the continent. The term soon became popular. The idea of manifest destiny combined a practical government policy with Americans' belief that God supported their right to westward expansion. Expansionists used the phrase to support annexation of Texas and Oregon.

After negotiations supported by President Polk, the United States and Britain signed a treaty in 1846 that split Oregon Country at the 49° line. Farther east, this was already the existing boundary between the United States and Canada. Land south of the line became Oregon Territory. The land north of the line became part of British Columbia, Canada.

With Texas and Oregon now inside the United States' territory, expansionists looked toward the Pacific coast to expand. California, a part of Mexico since 1822, was the prize. Before they could gain possession of California, however, the United States had to acquire the land between California and Texas.

The Mexican War

Mexico did not want to sell the territory, so the United States concluded that it must be conquered through war. It was given an excuse to start fighting when, in 1846, Mexican troops crossed the Rio Grande and attacked some American soldiers. In response, President Polk quickly asked Congress to declare war, which it did.

American forces did not win as easily as Polk anticipated. And not all Americans supported the war with Mexico. In 1846, the Whigs gained control of Congress and joined with antiwar Democrats to oppose Polk's policies. The Whigs, especially those from New England, feared that the war was an excuse to spread slavery even farther, beyond Texas. Some people claimed that the North had nothing to fear because cotton could not grow in the region. Northern abolitionists knew, however, that slavery had been used to grow many other crops and even prospered in cities. Slavery, in some form, could spread into the Southwest and abolitionists felt this had to be prevented.

The Mexican War continued for two years. The American army, led by General Zachary Taylor, gradually conquered

"Mexico is to us the forbidden fruit; the penalty of defeating it would be to subject our institutions to political death."

Senator John Calhoun, 1846

The Battle of Palo Alto was the first battle of the Mexican War. On May 8, 1846, General Zachary Taylor and about 2,300 troops met a Mexican force of 6,000, which had come north across the Rio Grande. After a five-hour battle, superior American weapons won the day, and the Mexicans retreated.

much of northeastern Mexico. General Winfield Scott then used the United States Navy to move more than 14,000 troops down the Mexican coast to Vera Cruz. They then marched toward Mexico City, which they captured in September 1848.

Meanwhile, in June 1846, Americans in California staged a rebellion known as the Bear Flag Revolt. The rebellion took its name from the bear on the flag raised by rebels when they seized the town of Sonoma, California. Californians declared themselves independent of Mexico and established the Republic of California, or Bear Flag Republic. The explorer John Charles Frémont was chosen as the republic's leader on July 5, 1846.

The New Territories

The Mexican War came to an end with the Treaty of Guadalupe Hidalgo in 1848. In this treaty, Mexico gave up the northern part of its territory—all of what are now New Mexico and California, and parts of present-day Arizona, Colorado, Nevada, and Utah. Mexico also gave up its claims to Texas. In return, the United States paid Mexico $15 million.

California, now United States territory, organized a territorial government in 1849 and adopted a constitution that forbade slavery. The territory asked Congress to be admitted to the Union as a state, but was prevented by the slavery issue. There were 30 states in the Union, 15 proslavery and 15 antislavery. If California entered the Union as a free state, it would upset the balance.

Other issues also troubled Congress. The New Mexico and Utah territories needed their futures determined. Southerners wanted laws that allowed them to take slaves into the new territories. They said the North was denying them their rights in these regions.

The Wilmot Proviso and 1848 Election

The United States had succeeded in winning vast new lands, but the political battles within the nation continued. During

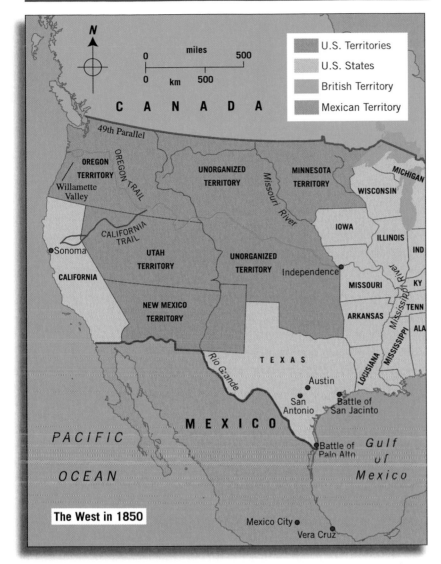

The ideal of Manifest Destiny had led the United States to great expansion of its territories by 1850. From Oregon in the Northwest, through California and the new territories of Utah and New Mexico, to the huge region of Texas—all were now American territory.

The West in 1850

the Mexican War, Congress debated a bill to pay for lands the United States might gain from Mexico. In August 1846, Representative David Wilmot from Pennsylvania, a Democrat, introduced an amendment to the bill, saying that no land acquired from Mexico should ever allow slavery. This proposed amendment was known as the Wilmot Proviso.

President Polk's supporters in the House of Representatives tried to limit the Wilmot Proviso to lands north of the line 36°30', which was the boundary stated in the Missouri Compromise. The House passed Wilmot's bill, but the Senate

The California Gold Rush

In January 1848, gold was discovered by American settlers in California. The California Gold Rush that followed drew thousands of gold seekers, or prospectors, to the region. It sped up the pace of westward migration and led to California coming under American control.

Newspapers across the globe carried stories about prospectors who struck it rich digging for gold. Australian, Chinese, European, and Mexican people all made their way to California. By 1852, more than 250,000 people of various nationalities had settled in California. At the time, the California Gold Rush was producing nearly half of the nation's gold supply. For some prospectors, this meant realizing the dreams that had brought them west. But only a few struck it rich. Most settlers failed to find gold and took work as farmers or manual laborers for large mining companies.

In 1850, California passed the Foreign Miners Tax to push foreigners out of the gold mining business. Other laws prevented blacks, Indians, and Chinese from receiving education or testifying in court. Of all the ethnic groups in the region, Indians suffered the worst. Gold prospectors took advantage of Native Americans and used violence to force them into labor. As a result, many Indians fled the region. Others died from diseases brought to the region by the new settlers. California's native population went from 150,000 in 1848 to only 25,000 in 1856.

Chinese gold prospectors in California during the Gold Rush.

did not. Wilmot then introduced another antislavery bill. This also passed in the House but not the Senate. The Wilmot Proviso never became law, but it did not disappear.

By the time of the 1848 presidential campaign, the Democratic party was torn apart by opposing groups. The Northern Democrats who wanted to abolish slavery split from the main party and held their own meeting, where they formed the Free-Soil party. The term "free soil" came from the party's belief that all American lands, or soil, should be free of slavery. This new party supported the Wilmot Proviso and nominated Martin Van Buren for president. Van Buren, who had been president from 1837 to 1841, pulled many voters away from the Democratic candidate, Martin Cass. The Democrats and Cass continued to support the idea that states should decide the slavery issue for themselves.

The Whigs, who already had a majority in Congress, had as their candidate the popular war hero Zachary Taylor. He had been a soldier his whole adult life and seldom expressed his political opinions. But Taylor liked the idea of running for president, and accepted the Whig nomination. Taylor's popularity in the nation won him the presidency.

The Wilmot Proviso, meanwhile, had aroused the fears and outrage of Southerners. In the Senate, John Calhoun defended the Southern position. The Western territories belonged to the entire Union, he stated, and therefore the laws of every state should be honored in the territories.

The Compromise of 1850

Henry Clay proposed solving the argument with a series of compromises. The Compromise of 1850, as the complicated deal became known, was a political masterpiece. Clay knew that the issues covered by the Compromise, if included in a single bill, would fail to pass in Congress. Separately, however, each part of the plan could

Zachary Taylor, seen here outside his tent during the Mexican War, was chosen by the Whig party as their presidential candidate in 1848. His victories in the recent war helped him to victory in the presidential election.

obtain a majority vote. Therefore, Clay introduced five separate bills to Congress.

First, Congress voted to admit California as a free state. Second, the Texas and New Mexico Act organized New Mexico as a territory. Popular sovereignty, or the right of citizens in an area to decide whether or not to allow slavery, would let New Mexico choose its own position on slavery when it became a state. The Act also allowed the United States to pay Texas $10 million if it gave up any Texan claim to New Mexico. Third, another act declared that Utah would also decide for itself about making slavery legal. Fourth, Congress passed a Fugitive Slave Act that put runaway slaves under government control. This law allowed U.S. officials to return runaway slaves to their owners without jury trials. It also declared that anyone who aided a fugitive slave could be arrested and fined. Finally, Congress abolished

The Compromise of 1850 tried to resolve the problem of slavery in the states and territories, and to find a compromise between the interests of the North and the South. But the fragile balance between slave states and free states had moved west into new territories, and the dispute continued.

The United States after the Compromise of 1850

Free States and Territories
Slave States and Territories

the slave trade in Washington, D.C. Slaves could no longer be bought or sold in the nation's capital.

For his efforts in making the Compromise of 1850, Henry Clay was called "The Great Pacificator," or peacemaker. Clay's peace did not last very long, however. Northern abolitionists immediately said they would defy the Fugitive Slave Act. For the first time, they planned to take direct action against federal officials. Southerners claimed that Northerners were going to sabotage the Compromise.

Hispanics in America

Today, the United States is home to over 22 million Hispanic people. Many are descendants of recent Mexican immigrants or Mexicans who lived in the Southwest when it was annexed by the United States in 1845. The two other largest Hispanic groups are Puerto Ricans and Cubans. Still others have come from throughout Latin America.

At least 80,000 Mexicans lived in the southwestern regions acquired by the United States after the Mexican War. Most of them received American citizenship in the years that followed. Still, they retained their language, foods, religion, and customs.

During the twentieth century, millions of Hispanics entered the United States. Between 1910 and 1930, the Mexican Revolution pushed more than 600,000 Mexicans into the nation. In the middle of the century, half a million Puerto Ricans came to America. Many settled in East Harlem in New York City. Most Cubans came after Fidel Castro took power in Cuba in 1959. By 1975, about 500,000 Cubans had fled to the United States, many ending up in Miami, Florida. In 1980, yet another wave of 125,000 Cubans came to America, 80,000 of whom settled in Miami.

The United States government has repeatedly tried to restrict Hispanic immigration. In the 1930s, nearly 500,000 Mexicans, some of them United States citizens, were sent back to Mexico. In the 1950s, another 3.8 million Hispanics were deported in an attempt to reduce the number of illegal immigrants. In 1994, President Bill Clinton announced that the United States would no longer allow in refugees from Cuba. Even so, Hispanics still account for one-third of America's immigrants.

7

The Union Comes Apart

This 1851 antislavery poster expresses opposition to the Fugitive Slave Act in Boston, Massachusetts. Northerners were outraged at the rights given to commissioners. These government officials could order anyone to help them enforce the law and could punish those who helped escaped slaves.

The Compromise of 1850 tried to solve the sectional problems in the United States. But it also overturned the balance that had been established in the Missouri Compromise. The next decade proved that the division between North and South was too great to bridge.

Opposition to the Compromise

Southerners were angered by the Compromise of 1850 for three reasons. First, federal law no longer declared that slavery had a right to expand. Popular sovereignty rather than a geographic line would determine the legality of slavery. Second, it pushed the balance away from the South by admitting California as a free state. Third, it limited the ability of Southerners to buy or sell slaves within the United States. This, they believed, would lead to more limitations in the future.

Northerners also disliked the Compromise of 1850, and for some of the same reasons. First, it broke the Missouri Compromise. No longer would the geographic line of 36°30' place limits on the extension of slavery. Instead, the legality of slavery would be decided in elections. Second, it made it illegal for anyone to help slaves escape to freedom. The Fugitive Slave Act made it a federal crime to aid a runaway slave and it ordered Northern law officers to help return

FUGITIVE SLAVE BILL!

HON. HENRY WILSON

Will address the citizens on

Thursday Evening, April 3,

At the

At 7 o'clock, on the all-engrossing topics of the day—the FUGITIVE SLAVE BILL, the pro-slavery action of the National Government and the general aspect of the Slavery question.

Let every man and woman, without distinction of sect or party, attend the meeting and bear a testimony against the system which fills the prisons of a free republic with men whose only crime is a love of freedom—which strikes down the habeas corpus and trial by jury, and converts the free soil of Massachusetts into hunting ground for the Southern kidnappers.

Ashby, March 29, 1851.

White & Potter's Steam Press—4000 Impressions per hour—Spring Lane, Boston.

The Underground Railroad

During the antebellum era, thousands of slaves from the South escaped to the free states in the North, to Canada, or to Indian territories. Reaching freedom was not an easy task. Southern towns used local militias to patrol the countryside, and black people were not allowed to travel without passes. Bounties, or rewards, encouraged people to capture and return runaways. Nevertheless, slaves used clever means to find their way to freedom. Henry "Box" Brown, in perhaps the most cunning of escapes, shipped himself north in a wooden crate marked "This side up with care."

Many slaves escaped through a system called the Underground Railroad. This network of antislavery sympathizers provided hiding places, food, directions, and transportation to runaway slaves. Only on rare occasions did the Underground Railroad actually use the railroads. Slaves often walked most of their way to freedom. Although some whites participated in the network, the Underground Railroad mainly connected the homes, churches, and neighborhoods of free blacks in the South.

Those who helped the slaves were known as "conductors" on the Underground Railroad. Harriet Tubman, a former slave herself, was a leading conductor. She helped between 300 and 400 slaves in their escape to freedom in the North. Tubman tried to use a different path on each of her journeys and did most of her traveling at night.

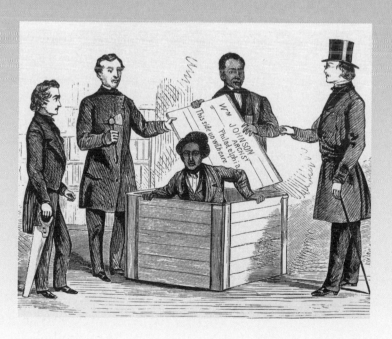

Henry "Box" Brown arrives in Philadelphia from the South.

runaways. For many abolitionists, the Fugitive Slave Act was the most horrible element of the Compromise.

The Fugitive Slave Act

The Fugitive Slave Act was designed to protect the financial interests of Southern slave owners. It created special officials who could arrest fugitive slaves and then issue documents to let their owners reclaim them. Although this was a court procedure, the fugitive slaves were not permitted jury trials, nor were they given the right to testify on their own behalf. The officials, on the other hand, were given great powers.

Despite harsh consequences, some abolitionists formed committees to rescue fugitive slaves and to protect them against being returned to their owners. They hid runaway slaves in their attics, forged papers that said slaves were free blacks, and helped the slaves reach Canada. Hundreds of abolitionists were fined or jailed for their opposition to the Fugitive Slave Act.

Perhaps the most famous abolitionist response to the Fugitive Slave Act was a novel written by Harriet Beecher Stowe. *Uncle Tom's Cabin; or, Life Among the Lowly* was originally published in 36 parts in the antislavery newspaper *National Era*. When it was published as a book in 1852, it became an immediate success. Over a million copies of the book were sold by 1856. Although Stowe had never visited the South, many Northerners believed that she had accurately captured the cruel realities of Southern slavery.

Violence in Kansas

The Compromise of 1850 had introduced the idea of popular sovereignty into government. This caused problems that exploded in Kansas Territory in 1854. In January of that year, Stephen A. Douglas, a Democratic senator from Illinois, introduced a bill to organize the territories of Kansas and Nebraska. Popular sovereignty, the bill stated, would let the region's citizens decide whether slavery would be allowed in their territories. Despite opposition, Douglas's bill became law.

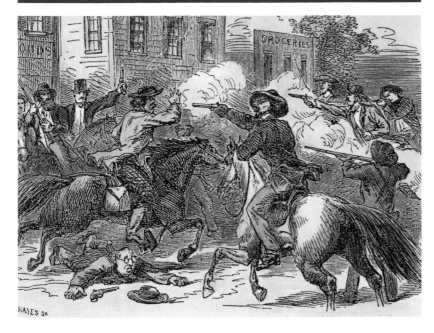

HAYES sc

By 1856, proslavery supporters had established a territorial government in Lecompton, Kansas, and abolitionists had set up their own legislature in Lawrence, Kansas. Lawrence, seen here, was looted by a mob of proslavery Kansas men and Border Ruffians on May 21, 1856.

Kansas Territory soon became the place where the proslavery and antislavery forces clashed. Thousands of slave owners and abolitionists from across the nation came to vote in local elections in Kansas. Missouri Senator David Atchinson led hundreds of proslavery Missouri men—called "Border Ruffians"—across state lines and to the Kansas polls. Supported by the New England Emigrant Aid Society, many abolitionists also traveled to and voted in Kansas.

In the months that followed, Northerners and Southerners in Kansas held competing state constitutional conventions, won separate elections, and organized independent governments. President Franklin Pierce recognized the proslavery legislature in Lecompton, Kansas, and warfare quickly resulted. Antislavery campaigners protested, and in May 1856, some 700 proslavery men attacked Lawrence, Kansas, looting and destroying abolitionist newspaper offices, stores, and buildings.

Abolitionists in the North were horrified. Massachusetts Senator Charles Sumner responded to the violence with a fiery speech called "The Crime Against Kansas." He said the Lecompton legislature was illegal and questioned the actions

John Brown (1800–59)

John Brown was born in Connecticut and spent his childhood in Ohio. He tried but failed at several businesses before moving to Kansas in 1855. There, his antislavery feelings made him known as one of the most outspoken abolitionists in America.

Brown threw himself into the fight when the Kansas-Nebraska Act was passed. After murdering five proslavery settlers along Pottawatomie Creek, Brown justified his actions on the grounds that he was doing God's work.

Although the murders horrified most Americans, Brown's willingness to use violence to end slavery met with approval among some abolitionists. With this newfound support, Brown planned to overthrow slavery entirely. His supporters provided him with money and supplies. On October 16, 1859, Brown made an attack on Harper's Ferry, Virginia.

Brown was captured, charged with treason, and sentenced to hang. In the days before his execution, Brown became a hero to abolitionists. They declared the justness of his actions and warned that his would not be the only attack on slavery. On his way to the gallows, Brown gave a note to a jailer that foresaw the violent future that would result from the slavery issue.

of President Pierce. He defended abolition and criticized Southerners for their cruel treatment of slaves.

Sumner's speech outraged many Southerners. It also resulted in blood being shed in Congress. On May 21, 1856, Sumner was approached by Congressman Preston Brooks of South Carolina. Brooks yelled at the elder statesman and then proceeded to strike him over his head with a walking cane. The beating ended with Sumner on the Senate floor.

John Brown, a Northern-born abolitionist, took revenge against the proslavery activists in Kansas. The day after the caning of Sumner, Brown and seven others proclaimed themselves to be the "Army of the North." They forced themselves into the cabins of three proslavery families in Pottawatomie Creek in Kansas. When the Pottawatomie Massacre ended, Brown and his men had split the skulls of or otherwise mutilated five men.

New Antislavery Parties

The opposition to the Kansas-Nebraska Act in the North resulted in the creation of new political parties that declared their absolute opposition to the further extension of slavery. One was the Know-Nothing, party, which opposed Roman Catholicism, immigrants, and slavery. The Free-Soil party also attracted Northern voters by claiming that slavery threatened the nation's republican institutions.

By 1854, the newly-created Republican party was attracting many Know-Nothings, Free-Soilers, and Northern Whigs and Democrats. (This was not the same party as the old Republican party, or Democratic-Republicans, part of

This cartoon from about 1850 supports the "Know-Nothings" by showing an Irish immigrant (in the whiskey barrel) and a German immigrant (in the beer barrel) stealing a ballot box during an election. Know-Nothings were against slavery, but they were also against the European immigrants who, they believed, were taking over their country.

79

which had become the Democratic party in the 1820s.) The Republicans' first national meeting, in Ripon, Wisconsin, called for the repeal of both the Kansas-Nebraska Act and the Fugitive Slave Law. The party quickly attracted supporters throughout the North. In 1854, Republican candidates won several state and local elections.

In 1856, the Republican party nominated John Frémont as its first presidential candidate. Frémont was 43 years old and a hero in California. He had led the Bear Flag Revolt in 1846 and was one of California's first senators. His slogan was "Free Speech, Free Press, Free Soil, Free Men, and Frémont." The Know-Nothing party and the Whig party held separate conventions, but nominated the same candidate, the former president Millard Fillmore.

The Democratic party branded Frémont as a threat to the Union. Republicans, they claimed, were determined to create bad feeling between the North and South, and cared only for Northern interests. The Democrats offered instead James Buchanan, from Pennsylvania, as their presidential candidate.

Buchanan won the election and Frémont came in second. The Republicans, however, were optimistic about their results. Republicans had won seats in the House and in the Senate, as well as filling many local positions throughout the North. They had proved that the Republicans were a powerful political party. To Southerners, Republican successes were a bad sign. They felt their way of life was being threatened even more by the North.

The Dred Scott Decision

As the 1850s progressed, federal laws and court decisions continued to support the right to own slaves. In 1857, the Supreme Court made its most proslavery decision yet. Dred Scott was a slave who belonged to Dr. John Emerson, an army surgeon from Missouri. Emerson took Scott to Illinois for two years and then to Wisconsin, where slavery was forbidden under the Missouri Compromise, for two more years. When Dr. Emerson died, his widow inherited Scott.

Frederick Douglass (1817–95)

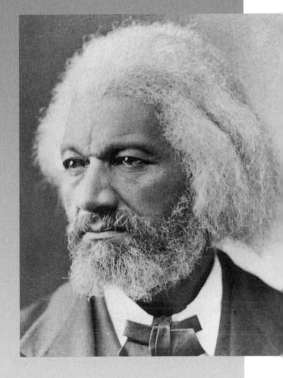

One of the most well-known former slaves who fought for freedom was Frederick Douglass. He was born a slave in Maryland in about 1817, but escaped from captivity when he was 21. He made his way to Massachusetts, thanks to a free African American who gave him forged papers that said he was a seaman. There, Douglass saw for the first time a copy of the abolitionist newspaper *The Liberator*. A few years later, he became a speaker for the Massachusetts Antislavery Society and was soon a famous abolitionist.

In 1845, Douglass published his *Narrative of the Life of Frederick Douglass*. This book made Douglass so famous that he risked being captured and returned to slavery. To avoid this, he spent the next two years lecturing in Britain. With the help of British friends, he bought his freedom and returned to the United States. Douglass settled in Rochester, New York, and became editor of an abolitionist newspaper, the *North Star*. He named the newspaper after the star that many slaves followed on their trips to freedom. He ran the paper for 17 years.

During the Civil War, Douglass worked to enlist men in African American regiments. After the war, he held several government positions, finally as United States minister to Haiti from 1889 to 1891.

In 1846, Scott sued Mrs. Emerson in a Missouri court for his freedom, claiming that he was free because he had lived in free territories. The Missouri circuit court agreed, but the Missouri Supreme Court overturned the decision. Scott remained a slave even though he had lived on free soil between 1834 and 1838. The case then went to the Supreme Court of the United States.

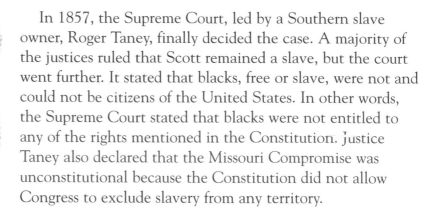

In 1857, the Supreme Court, led by a Southern slave owner, Roger Taney, finally decided the case. A majority of the justices ruled that Scott remained a slave, but the court went further. It stated that blacks, free or slave, were not and could not be citizens of the United States. In other words, the Supreme Court stated that blacks were not entitled to any of the rights mentioned in the Constitution. Justice Taney also declared that the Missouri Compromise was unconstitutional because the Constitution did not allow Congress to exclude slavery from any territory.

"I hold that, under the Constitution of the United States, each State of this Union has a right to do as it pleases on the subject of slavery..... It is none of our business whether slavery exists in Missouri or not."

Stephen A. Douglas, Lincoln-Douglas Debates, 1858

The Lincoln-Douglas Debates

In 1858, Stephen Douglas, the senator from Illinois who had introduced the Kansas-Nebraska Act in 1854, ran for reelection. He believed popular sovereignty could still work in spite of the Dred Scott ruling. His opponent in the Illinois election was a political newcomer, Republican Abraham Lincoln.

Lincoln's strategy was to oppose slavery, but not to offend slave owners. In his speech accepting the Republican nomination at the party's Illinois state convention, he said that slavery would inevitably end because "a house divided against itself cannot stand." Still, Lincoln said that he did not believe that the United States could do anything to end slavery where it already existed.

Lincoln challenged Douglas to a series of seven debates across the state of Illinois. Douglas accepted, and huge crowds came to hear the two speakers. Part of the attraction was the difference between the two men. Douglas was only about five feet tall, fiery, and sophisticated. People called

The Democrat Stephen Douglas was Abraham Lincoln's opponent in the 1858 election for senator from Illinois. He was not opposed to slavery on moral grounds, as Lincoln was. However, he said that popular sovereignty should give people the right to exclude slavery from their territories if they so wished.

Abraham Lincoln (1809–65)

Abraham Lincoln was born in Kentucky. His family moved several times within Kentucky and then to Illinois. Lincoln was mostly self-educated: He claimed to have had less than one year's formal schooling, but he loved to read in his spare time.

Lincoln studied law and then moved to Springfield, Illinois. There he met and married Mary Todd, with whom he had four sons. Lincoln served four terms in the state legislature, one term in Congress (from 1847 to 1849), and then became a full-time attorney.

Lincoln reentered politics in 1854. Even though he lost the 1858 election in Illinois, he gained national attention and, in 1860, Lincoln was elected president of the United States. His election outraged many Southerners. By the time he took office, seven states had already seceded from the Union. In 1861, the Civil War began. A total of 11 states declared their independence, and Lincoln fought to preserve the Union.

Lincoln gradually turned the war for the Union into a war against slavery. On January 1, 1863, he issued the Emancipation Proclamation, which declared freedom for the slaves in the South. This united the cause of abolition with that of the preservation of the Union. The Civil War was long and bloody, victories were costly, and support for Lincoln dropped in the North. But when General Sherman captured Atlanta in September 1864, Lincoln's popularity soared. The North was going to win the war.

Just as the war was ending, Lincoln was assassinated by John Wilkes Booth, who shot him at a theater in Washington, D.C. Lincoln died on April 15, 1865.

"A house divided against itself cannot stand. . . . I believe this government cannot endure permanently half slave and half free. I do not expect the Union to be dissolved; I do not expect the house to fall; but I do expect it will cease to be divided. It will become all one thing, or all the other."

Abraham Lincoln, 1858

"I John Brown am now quite certain that the crimes of this guilty land will never be purged away, but with blood."

John Brown, just before his execution, December 2, 1859

him "the little giant." In contrast, Lincoln was tall and thin. He played up his poor childhood and his birth in a log cabin. Some of the debates lasted for hours, as onlookers listened intently to the issues.

Lincoln used the debates as an opportunity to attack slavery. Although he did not say he believed in racial equality, Lincoln expressed the belief that blacks deserved basic human rights. They had "the right to eat the bread, without leave of anybody else, which his own hand earns." Douglas won reelection, but Lincoln emerged as a national figure.

Harper's Ferry

On both sides of the sectional divide, feelings and actions became stronger and angrier. In October 1859, abolitionist John Brown led a heavily armed team of 18 men and seized the federal arsenal at Harper's Ferry, Virginia. Brown was supported by abolitionists from the North. He planned to provide enough guns for a slave rebellion that would finally put an end to slavery and create a black republic in the South. However, United States soldiers under Colonel Robert E. Lee ended the assault on Harper's Ferry. Brown was captured and ten of his men were killed. Brown was charged with treason and sentenced to death. He was executed on December 2, 1859.

In response to the raid on Harper's Ferry and the Dred Scott decision, some Southerners became even more defensive of slavery. Senator Jefferson Davis of Mississippi tried to introduce a series of laws to protect slavery, but these were not passed. Many Southerners now believed that they would have to leave the United States altogether if they were to preserve slavery and the Southern way of life.

The 1860 Presidential Election

These difficult times resulted in the 1860 presidential election becoming a four-way race. The Democratic party split into Northern and Southern factions, each one nominating a candidate for president. Stephen Douglas received the Northern nomination—he promised to find a compromise on the slavery issue and keep the nation united. John C. Breckinridge received the Southern nomination and called for a government slavery code in the Western territories. The Republican party nominated Abraham Lincoln, who advocated free soil, a high tariff, and the right of each state to determine the status of slavery within its borders. The Constitutional Unionist party, which was composed mostly of Whigs and Know-Nothings, nominated John Bell of Tennessee. Their party was silent on the issue of slavery and simply stated, "the Constitution as it is and the Union as it is."

The fact that there were four choices for voters helped Lincoln win the presidency. He won a huge majority in the North, and Southern voters were split between the three other candidates. So even without any support in the slave states, Lincoln was elected as president.

By May 20, 1861, 11 states had seceded from the Union. South Carolina was the first to secede, in December 1860. It was joined in January and February 1861 by Mississippi, Florida, Alabama, Georgia, Louisiana, and Texas. In April and May, Virginia, Arkansas, Tennessee, and North Carolina also became Confederate states. The United States of America was united no longer.

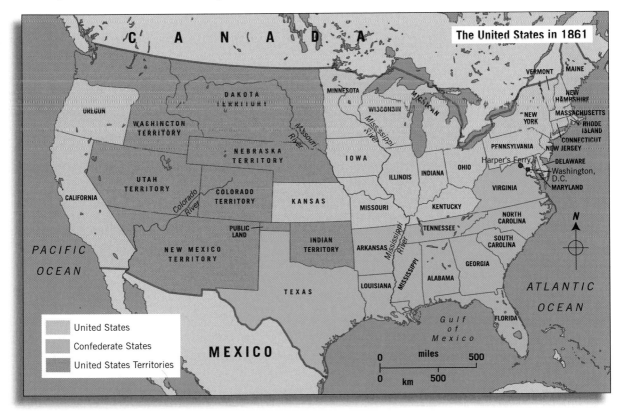

The United States in 1861

United States
Confederate States
United States Territories

Upon hearing the news of Lincoln's victory, outraged Southerners prepared to leave the Union. South Carolina seceded in December 1860. Ten other Southern states followed in the next few months, and together formed their own nation, the Confederate States of America. By the time Lincoln was inaugurated as president, on March 4, 1861, the Confederacy was a reality.

Third Parties

There is nothing in American law to say there should be only two major political parties in the United States. Nevertheless, in our nation's history there have usually been two major parties and smaller, often local, parties fighting to have their voices heard. Third-party candidates have yet to win a presidential election, but they have shaped political debates and the outcome of elections.

From 1832 to 1860, every presidential election had a third-party candidate. In each case, the candidate fared poorly. These failures, however, did not prevent the rise of new political parties after the Civil War. James Weaver received over a million votes in 1892 as the Populist party candidate. This result persuaded the Democratic party to run Populist William J. Bryan as its candidate in 1896 and 1900. Bryan did not win those elections, but he did bring new issues—those of the struggling farmer—to the front of American politics.

In the twentieth century, many third-party candidates ran for president in order to raise awareness about issues they believed the main parties neglected. Eugene Debs ran for president five times between 1900 and 1920 as the Socialist party candidate. In 1948, Henry Wallace, a former vice president under Franklin D. Roosevelt, gained more than a million votes as the presidential candidate for the Progressive party. More recently, Ross Perot, representing the Reform party, received 19 percent of the vote in 1992 and eight percent in 1996. His candidacy was credited for taking enough votes away from George Bush in 1992 to give Bill Clinton his victory.

Conclusion

By 1860, the antebellum era was nearly over. The United States had changed greatly since 1820. Huge territories had been added and the nation's western boundary now extended all the way to the Pacific Ocean. Industrial and transportation revolutions had transformed the way Americans lived and worked.

New industries and technology had reshaped the Northern economy. Reform movements, including temperance, women's rights, and abolitionism, had changed people's thinking. In the South, the cotton industry had expanded with the nation's borders and slavery had become even more important.

As the nation grew, however, it also divided. For some Southerners, slavery needed to be preserved at all costs. For radical abolitionists, slavery needed to be ended at all costs. Others believed that compromises were needed in order to preserve that which mattered most: the Union. As the antebellum era progressed, compromises became more difficult. Other issues also divided the nation. The idea of states' rights raised the question of whether the federal government or state governments were the supreme power.

Political compromises held North and South together until 1860, but in the end the institution of slavery split the nation apart. Northern abolitionists and Southern slave owners were unable to find positions that could satisfy them both. Their differing views led first to the secession of the Southern states and then, in 1861, to the Civil War.

In the terrible and violent years that followed, this division was fought out on battlefields throughout the United States. Nearly 600,000 Americans lost their lives in this war. This amounted to more American fatalities than in all other American wars combined.

Glossary

abolition   Getting rid of something, or the name of the movement to end slavery (also called *abolitionism*).

agriculture   The work of farmers, mostly growing crops and raising livestock for food.

annex   To take ownership of another nation or add territory to a nation.

arsenal   A store of weapons and ammunition.

commerce   The business of buying and selling things.

compromise   An agreement reached by negotiation between people or groups that is acceptable to both parties, even if it is not what they originally wanted.

constitution   The basic plan and principles of a government.

democratic   A system where people are their own authority rather than being ruled over by a monarch. In a democratic system, people vote on decisions and rules, or elect representatives to vote for them.

Democrats   The political party founded in the 1820s and in which Southerners who supported states' rights were very powerful for many years.

descendant   A person who comes after another person in the same family. It can mean a son or daughter, or someone hundreds of years later.

economics   To do with the production and use of goods and services, and the system of money that is used for the flow of goods and services.

economy   The system of money that is used for the flow of goods and services.

emancipation   The freeing of a person who has been a slave.

embargo   A government order to stop trade and transportation of goods between one country and another.

export   To send something abroad to sell or trade. An export is also the thing that is sent, such as tobacco or cotton.

federal   To do with the central, or national, government of a country rather than the regional or state governments.

feminist   To do with equality for women, or a person who believes in equality for women.

immigrant   A person who has left the country of his or her birth and come to live in another country.

import   To bring goods into a country. An import is also the thing that is brought in, such as tea or cloth.

legislation	Laws, or the making of laws.
legislature	An official group of people with the power to make laws, or the branch of government that makes laws.
militia	A locally organized military group.
monopoly	The ownership or control of a particular thing, or the supply of a particular thing, by one person or group.
nullification	Cancellation of something or making something of no value, especially in the case of states refusing to acknowledge United States laws.
petition	A paper signed by people asking a government body to take some action.
plantation	A farm where crops, such as tobacco or sugarcane, are grown, and where the work is done by large teams of workers. In the past, these workers were often slaves.
policy	A plan or way of doing things that is decided on, and then used in managing situations, making decisions, or tackling problems.
ratify	To approve. For example, the U.S. Senate must ratify treaties before they can go into effect.
repeal	To undo an earlier decision.
Republicans	The political party founded in 1854 to oppose the expansion of slavery.
reservation	An area of land set aside for Native American tribes whose homelands had been taken or reduced by white settlement.
resolution	A statement that declares the intention or opinion of an official group, such as a government body.
secede	To leave the Union. The act of leaving is called *secession*.
sectional	Something divided into sections, such as the political interests of people in different regions of a country.
suffrage	The right to vote.
tariff	A tax on imported goods.
technology	The knowledge and ability that improves ways of doing practical things. A person performing any task with a tool is using technology.
treaty	An agreement reached between two or more groups or countries after discussion and negotiation.
utopia	An imaginary and perfect place.

Time Line

1793	Cotton gin invented by Eli Whitney.
1807	Robert Fulton builds the steamboat *Clermont*.
	Congress passes Embargo Act.
1816	Second Bank of the United States founded.
1817	American Colonization Society formed.
1818	Andrew Jackson invades Florida in First Seminole War.
1819	Tallmadge Amendment.
	United States acquires Florida from Spain in Adams-Onís Treaty.
1820	Maine becomes a state.
1820–21	Congress passes Missouri Compromise.
1821	Missouri becomes a state.
1822	Liberia settled by African Americans.
1823	Monroe Doctrine.
1824	Henry Clay proposes "American System."
	John Quincy Adams elected president.
1825	Erie Canal opens.
1828	Congress passes "Tariff of Abominations."
	Andrew Jackson elected president.
1830	Congress passes Indian Removal Act.
1831	William Lloyd Garrison begins publishing *The Liberator*.
	Nat Turner's Rebellion.
1832	Andrew Jackson reelected president.
	Nullification crisis.
1833	Jackson removes federal deposits from Bank of the United States.
	American Antislavery Society formed.
	Congress passes Force Bill.
1834	Whig party forms.
1835	General López de Santa Anna takes control of Mexico.
1835–42	Second Seminole War.
1836	American Temperance Union holds first annual convention.
	Congress passes "gag rule."
	Texans declare independence from Mexico.
	Battle of the Alamo.
	Battle of San Jacinto.

1839   *Amistad* uprising.
1840   William Henry Harrison elected president.
1841   John Tyler becomes president upon death of President Harrison.
1842   Oregon Trail opens.
1843   Dorothea Dix reports on asylums, jails, and poorhouses in Massachusetts.
1844   James Polk elected president.
1845   Potato famine in Ireland results in huge emigration to United States.
        Texas becomes a state.
1846   Maine becomes first state to pass temperance law.
        Oregon Treaty signed by United States and Britain.
        Bear Flag Revolt establishes Republic of California.
        Wilmot Proviso proposed in Congress.
        Mexican War begins.
1848   Women's rights meeting held in Seneca Falls.
        Treaty of Guadalupe Hidalgo ends Mexican War.
        Zachary Taylor elected president.
1849   California Gold Rush begins.
1850   California becomes a state.
        Congress passes Compromise of 1850, including Fugitive Slave Act.
1854   Republican party forms.
        Congress passes Kansas-Nebraska Act.
1856   Violence erupts in Kansas, including Pottawatomie Massacre.
        James Buchanan elected president.
1857   Dred Scott decision made by Supreme Court.
1858   Lincoln-Douglas Debates.
1859   John Brown's raid on Harper's Ferry.
1860   Abraham Lincoln elected president.
        South Carolina secedes from the Union.
1861   11 Southern states form Confederate States of America.

Further Reading

Cullen-Dupont, Kathryn. *Elizabeth Cady Stanton & Women's Liberty* (Makers of America Series). New York: Facts on File, 1992.

Herda, D. J. *The Dred Scott Case: Slavery & Citizenship*. Springfield, NJ: Enslow, 1994.

Katz, William L. *Breaking the Chains: African-American Slave Resistance*. New York: Simon & Schuster, 1998.

McComb, David G. *Texas: An Illustrated History* (Oxford Illustrated Histories Series). New York: Oxford University Press, 1995.

Meltzer, Milton. *Andrew Jackson: And His America.* Danbury, CT: Watts, 1993.

Sherrow, Victoria. *Life During the Gold Rush* (Way People Live Series). San Diego, CA: Lucent Books, 1998.

Stowe, Harriet Beecher. *Uncle Tom's Cabin: or Life Among the Lowly*. Madison, WI: Demco, 1981.

Websites

Underground Railroad: Special Resource Study – This study includes a general overview of the Underground Railroad, with a brief discussion of slavery and abolitionism, escape routes used by slaves, and alternatives for commemoration and interpretation of the significance of this episode in American history.
www.nps.gov/undergroundrr

The New York State Canal System: Erie, Champlain, Oswego, and Cayuga – The official website of the New York State Canal System, published by the New York State Canal Corporation. This site contains canal-related activities and events and boating information.
www. canals.state.ny.us/

The National Women's History Project – The official website of the National Women's Originator of Women's History Month. Clearinghouse for U.S. women's history information.
www.nwhp.org/

Bibliography

Abzug, Robert. *Cosmos Crumbling: American Reform and the Religious Imagination*. New York: Oxford University Press, 1994.

The African American Mosaic: Library of Congress Resource Guide for the Study of Black History and Culture. Library of Congress website.

Barney, William L. *Passage of the Republic: An Interdisciplinary History of Nineteenth-Century America*. Lexington, MA: Heath, 1987.

Foner, Eric. *Free Soil, Free Labor, Free Men: The Ideology of the Republican Party Before the Civil War*. New York: Oxford University Press, 1995.

Frank, Andrew K. *Routledge Historical Atlas of the American South*. New York: Routledge Press, 1999.

Freehling, William. *The Road to Disunion: Secessionists at Bay, 1776–1854*. New York: Oxford University Press, 1991.

Gomez, Michael A. *Exchanging Our Country Marks: The Transformation of African Identities in the Colonial and Antebellum South*. Chapel Hill, NC: University of North Carolina Press, 1998.

Grolier Multimedia Encyclopedia. Danbury, CT: Grolier Interactive Inc., 1997.

Jeffrey, Julie Roy. *Frontier Women: The Trans-Mississippi West, 1840–1880*. New York: Hill and Wang, 1979.

Johnson, Paul E. *Shopkeeper's Millennium: Society and Revivals in Rochester, New York, 1815–1837*. New York: Hill and Wang, 1979.

King, Wilma. *Stolen Childhood: Slave Youth in Nineteenth-Century America*. Bloomington, IN: Indiana University Press, 1995.

Kolchin, Peter. *American Slavery: 1619–1877*. New York: Hill and Wang, 1994.

Linder, Doug. *The Amistad Case*. University of Missouri Law School website.

Morris, Richard B. and Henry Steele Commager, eds. *Encyclopedia of American History*. New York: Harper & Brothers, 1961.

Sellers, Charles. *The Market Revolution: Jacksonian America 1815–1846*. New York: Oxford University Press, 1994.

Thomas, Hugh. *Slavery*. New York: Simon & Schuster, 1997.

Index